PADDY AND THE BANSHEE
A Mythical Memoir Unlike Any Other

Don't Let the Bad Days Win!

Marty Martin

Content Warning: Contains sensitive subject matter, mature themes, mental health topics, violence and sexual content.

Little Elephant Publishing

martymartin.net

ISBN - Paperback: 978-1-955129-50-3
ISBN - Hardcover: 978-1-955129-56-5
ISBN - Ebook: 978-1-955129-51-0
ISBN - Audiobook : 978-1-955129-52-7

Published by: Little Elephant Publishing - St. Louis, Missouri

Edited by Karen L. Tucker
https://commaqueenediting.com/

Cover Art by Kat Powell
https://www.katpowellartist.com/

Interior Design by Kindlepreneur
https://kindlepreneur.com/book-formatting/

Photography credits:
All photographs courtesy of the author, public domain, or otherwise noted.
The JFK Library Archives https://www.jfklibrary.org/
Freepik.com
Dom DeLuise: https://www.wikipedia.org/
Jamie Lee Curtis photographs courtesy of Alan Light:
Walt Frazier: https://www.wikipedia.org/
https://yorkvillestoopstonuts.blogspot.com/

For more information contact:
Marty@martymartin.net
Martymartin.net

Printed in the United States of America

CONTENTS

DEDICATION

Dedicated to the little sister left behind and their mother for her gift of life and the sacrifices she made for Paddy and his sister.

AN INTRODUCTION

Paddy and Banshee is a different kind of autobiographical memoir; unlike any others you might find. The story blends a bit of imagination with the true story of six-year-old Paddy and his life in New York City, Ireland, and back again to New York in the 1960s. Paddy's imagination aside, everything in the story is true and did happen.

You may find it to be both entertaining and somewhat heartbreaking, and you may wonder how do Banshees fit into a memoir? The answer is simple when the memoir centers on a period in a child's life when a Banshee was a part of that child's experience, be it real or imagined. To omit the Banshee part of the story would be to erase an important part of Paddy's experience.

In life, there can be wonderment on how certain people, like Paddy, faced with so many life events and experiences in their young life, survived. It's unfortunate that children can fall victim to scary stories, illusions, and delusions, and occasionally the exercising of their own vivid and wild imaginations. Life can be cruel for a child, and the events a child experiences can leave a lasting impression, especially when personal heartbreak intertwines with encounters with Banshees and near misses with the Grim Reaper.

This story about Paddy is true, as true as a story can be as told by a sixty-something-year-old grandfather named Paddy, who when reflecting on that time in his young life, even with the advantage of time and adulthood, cannot shake the experiences of his six- to ten-year-old self when he lived in rural Kilkenny County, Ireland, in the 1960s.

The boy's name may not really be Paddy, but to tell this story, a hint of Irishness and anonymity may be necessary. Plus, Paddy is a good Irish name for a real boy who to this day as a father and grandfather might still believe Banshees are real.

If you are looking for a memoir or semi-autobiographical type of scary story possessing *some sort of literary genius*, you have not found it. If you're looking to have the bejesus scared out of you, you probably haven't found that either, unless you happen to already believe in Banshees. However, if you're interested in how a young boy from New York City at six years old ended up in the middle of Ireland and learned that Banshees are real while also managing to navigate and survive a broken home and a variety of other early-life challenges, well then, you may have found that story.

This story is about a young boy who grew up believing Banshees are real, and if he sees a comb on the sidewalk or laying on the ground, he will take a deliberate, nervous detour to avoid it and look over his shoulder, just to be sure nothing's there. On the rare occasion when he observes a female figure, young or old, with a striking resemblance to a distant memory, he still gets chills. Some may doubt the existence of Banshees, Grim Reapers, or Guardian Angels, but in the mind of a child's imagination, anything is possible, even that the imagined turns out to be very, very real.

WHAT'S A BANSHEE?

To fully understand the Banshee part of Paddy's story, you need to know what a Banshee is. You may have even heard countless Banshee stories and tales of their origins. Legends tell the story that a Banshee is supposedly a supernatural being, a creation of Irish folklore that initiated with a custom of keening, or singing, at funerals. The Banshee may be described as an elderly woman with long hair, a grey cloak, and red eyes. Others describe her as a young woman or a middle-aged woman. She is thought to be a fairy or ghost who warns of death by emitting a wailing sound—a screeching or continuous high-pitched, mournful crying.

Banshees are known for wailing outside the door of a house where it is believed someone is near death, and they have been seen near graveyards and Irish ruins. There are many more stories and encounters with Banshees, including Paddy's.

Combs, yes, combs and hairbrushes are also connected to stories about Banshees. Some stories tell of the Banshee with a comb or one who has lost a comb coaxing an unsuspecting soul to hand over the comb, with refusal to comply resulting in a deafening shrieking from the Banshee or even of disappearance or death. Banshee stories are many, varying in details, although with eerie similarities relating to wailing, screeching, long-haired women, a sense of fear and disbelief, to say the least, and—oh yes—combs.

Of course, many of the stories are accompanied by classic story lines of a dark and stormy night, or the wind howling, fog encroaching, the sound of approaching footsteps or heavy breathing, being frozen with fear, or a variety of enticing verbiages that induce anxiety, fear, and suspense. Paddy's introduction to the classic stories of the Banshee were in a pre-engagement stage, lying in wait for the unsuspecting Paddy.

PART 1

PADDY'S STORY BEGINS

Paddy's story began in the United States, where he was born in Baltimore to an Irish mother and American father. His parents met and had their young courtship in London, England, where Paddy's father was stationed in the Army in the 1950s. They married and traveled to the United States, and Paddy was born in 1956 to be a fearless, mischievous, curious, and easily influenced young boy. Despite his tendency to be attracted to what others may find harmful, or even outright dangerous, in addition to the known precarious circumstances of his life, he experienced a lifetime of what some might consider angelic protection, even into adulthood.

The Late 1970s

Human beings are excellent practitioners of suppressing memories. It's a learned and practiced skill that takes, in many cases, a lifetime of persistent practice. A little over a decade after his emotional escape from Ireland, Paddy had grown up in New York City, suppressing any memories of his distant four years of perceived terror he believed he experienced in Ireland. He attended Catholic schools, grew into a young man, joined the army, and married. Life was good for Paddy. Escape from Ireland some ten or twelve years earlier was a distant and suppressed memory until...

Paddy lay in bed sound asleep with his wife in their military housing unit at Fort Bragg, North Carolina, his mind filled with a variety of dreams that he would not remember except for the beginning of a far-off, low-pitched moan, barely audible but yet clear and eerily familiar, a sound that stirred memories as the seconds echoed. Still asleep, the intensity of what became a continuous wail increased in pitch and volume and startled Paddy, waking him up.

Although he was not fully awake, Paddy nervously contemplated where the moaning was coming from. Within seconds, it became clear as the moan continued to grow louder and louder, transitioning to an eerie, chilling, blood-curdling wail, that came from his wife's throat. The drawn-out wailing grew longer and louder with each iteration.

"Honey, wake up! Honey, honey, wake up, wake up," he yelled as he shook his wife, her wailing growing louder,

louder, and louder. Like the building crescendo of an orchestra's climatic performance, the wailing continued, creating a sense of panic and concern as his attempts to awaken his wife grew more aggressive, to a point of physically moving and shaking her until, finally, the wailing concluded with a long, heavy sigh, a sigh that projected a sense of eeriness and uncertainty.

"You okay, okay?"

"Yeah, I'm fine... I'll be okay," she answered slowly, exhaustion in her voice as she laid back down and quickly fell back to sleep without discussing what had transpired.

The lack of conversation concerned Paddy, although we need to remember, he was fearless, a paratrooper in the army, but this event created suspicion in his mind as he lay against her back and held her close. He was unable to go back to sleep as he tried to shake the unexplained wailing that had come from his wife. He tried to ignore it, but the wailing scared him and stirred up suppressed memories. He told himself, "Don't be stupid, it was a bad dream." However, it wasn't the dream that scared him but the eerie familiarity and sudden awakening of what he had, until that moment, suppressed, forgotten, and prayed to God to never see or hear again.

A flush of memories exploded as he began to shiver. *What was that? Did she, could she have, it couldn't be, could it? Did the Banshee follow me here? That's impossible, isn't it? Or a ghost, possession of some kind? It's been ten years. I don't understand, God, I asked you, prayed and thanked you for getting me out of there. It doesn't make any sense. How could this be happening?*

Paddy's mumbling and shivering as if he had a fever finally woke his wife up.

"You're shivering, babe, what's wrong?"

Paddy was shivering so violently that he was unable to say anything except mumble. She turned around, faced him, and held him tight. Ten minutes later, Paddy had calmed down. They continued their embrace and began to relax as they held each other. Paddy ran his fingers through her hair.

"What's this? You got something in your hair."

"What?" she answered lightheartedly as she followed Paddy's hand to the side of her head.

After a brief second of searching, she found it.

"What the heck!" She laughed. "How'd that get there? I thought I'd lost it. Oh, that's so silly of me... It's just my comb, honey."

As the years passed, the unexplained wailing from his wife would return occasionally, without rhyme, reason, or explanation. Paddy and his wife were blessed with three children, each with their own distinct personalities. As they grew older, Paddy would tell them about his years in Ireland as a youngster, but he made a point to never tell his children stories of his Banshee encounters, memories of which were revived on the occasions of his wife's wailing. Some wailing sessions were more extensive than others, and Paddy developed a sense for anticipating an oncoming wail and would try—and was on occasion successful—to intercept and stop the wailing.

When they discussed the instances of wailing, Paddy and his wife never understood or found a cause for it. The absence of answers troubled Paddy at times, as he often questioned if his memory of the Banshee was real or maybe he was being haunted by a ghost. With the benefit of so-called maturity and age, Paddy would find himself recalling his childhood, analyzing it for clarity.

Paddy's Early Years

Paddy's earliest memories were of a house in the suburbs of Baltimore, a memory likely reinforced by the few minutes of home movies of the time that reflected a happy Paddy with his parents and the bar his dad had built in the basement, dubbed the Irish Pub, with assorted animals on the front.

Vague memories followed of occasions on a plane flight with his mother on a trip to Ireland on Pan American Airways. Paddy was very proud of the Pan Am wings he was given by the stewardess. After short visits to Ireland, they would return to New York.

The next assortment of blended memories occurred in an apartment in New York City. Paddy started kindergarten but couldn't recall much other than it was a Catholic school where he wore a uniform.

Demons at Work

Demon scouts started on Paddy early as they searched for souls for their demon master to torment and plant seeds of mischievousness and danger. The first occasion that Paddy's propensity for being fearless, impulsive, and impatient struck him at school on a rainy day. When school ended, Paddy donned his classic long yellow raincoat and hat, walked out the door of the school, and began his walk home on his own, deciding not to wait for his dad. Did he know where he was going? No, he did not, although in the mind of a six-year-old, he thought he knew where he was going.

Paddy set out in the downpour, sloshing his way down the sidewalk and crossing countless intersections, always watching for the green light and looking both ways. After several minutes of his six-year-old feet trudging through ankle-high water, he heard a familiar voice calling him—his dad, who was understandably a bit frightened but also relieved.

This spontaneous unguided and unsupervised adventure may have been the first indication that Paddy may have been under some sort of angelic protection. Of course, this was also an indication that Paddy was a child who needed to be carefully watched because of his fearless and curious nature and attraction to dangerous activities. This propensity was clear in adulthood when he joined the army and decided to become a paratrooper and jump out of perfectly good airplanes.

During that kindergarten year, there was a move to a new apartment and new school where they also wore uniforms, somewhere nearby in New Jersey. The attraction to danger—or influence by demons—followed Paddy, and he found himself with a new friend in a vacant industrial lot overlooking a highway, a highway that provided the perfect opportunity for mischief.

It's Raining Lumber

This part of the story is not humorous in the least. Paddy and his friend found access to an unlimited supply of lumber in the form of two-by-fours and thought it was a good idea to throw the pieces of wood onto the highway, raining lumber from the overpass, deliberately aiming at cars passing underneath.

The highly dangerous operation—and miraculously, no one was hurt—continued for half an hour until they noticed two men wearing suits approaching. Paddy and his friend made a feeble attempt to escape these two men, who were detectives. The detectives verbally and angrily chastised the boys and took them home. They walked Paddy and his friend up the flight of stairs of the three-story apartment building, stopping on the second floor and knocking on the door of Paddy's friend's apartment. The detective explained the occurrence of the incident to the mother of Paddy's friend, who upon hearing the story began an onslaught of verbally thrashing her son and the beginning of a beating that moved from the hallway to behind the slammed door of the apartment. The cries of Paddy's friend were heard throughout the building and probably in the neighborhood, which Paddy noticed brought a smile to the detectives' faces.

The next stop was the third floor and a knock on the door of Paddy's apartment. As his mother answered the door, the cries of his friend were still bellowing through the staircase. Paddy had anticipated he would face similar retribution from his mother when she heard what he had done.

The detectives explained what happened to his mother, and she sincerely apologized. She did not begin to beat Paddy in front of the detectives and assured them that he would be dealt with. There was an awkward momentary pause before the closing of the door. To Paddy, it seemed as if the detectives were waiting for the beating to begin and were disappointed as the door closed.

Paddy was expecting a beating, but he was not beaten or punished, although his mother employed some sort of psychology on him, resulting in guilt about what he had done, but other than that, no other consequences.

More Moves

Another move back to New York City was in store. Paddy's dad did not live with them in New Jersey nor at the new apartment. Paddy did see his dad on occasions like Christmas and a few times when his dad took him on a trip to Front Royal, Virginia, where his dad had grown up. Paddy had fond memories of those trips where he caught fireflies and worms for fishing with his dad. The fishing with his dad part was where Paddy, unlike many boys and grown men, discovered he did not have an appreciation for nor liked fishing, especially after the episode when the snake tried to enter the boat.

A short time later, there was another move to Poughkeepsie, New York, where his mother moved in with a lawyer. Paddy's timeline may be flawed, given his age, but he remembers attending kindergarten for a few months followed by warmer weather and going to a public pool during the summer months. He also remembered there was a delivery a few mornings a week by a milkman who delivered powdered donuts, orange juice, and of course, milk. A not-so-pleasant memory of Paddy's came from when he was playing with water pistols outside in the evening. He carried the lawyer's false teeth container filled with water to resupply his water pistol, a method that worked perfectly. However, when he heard the lawyer calling for him and arrived at the front door, the lawyer asked about the container and Paddy returned it. The lawyer yanked Paddy by the arm, performing some sort of summersault acrobatics that resulted in a bottom beating unheard of before by Paddy. Screaming, he finally attempted a desperate escape, running to his mother inside the house.

Whether another move had been planned or if the bottom beating invoked a motherly protection instinct, it seemed to Paddy that a short time later, he was awakened by his mother in the middle of the night and ushered out to a car. His mother drove them to New York City, arriving at sunrise, where they lived in another apartment.

In the fall of 1962, the six-year-old Paddy found himself on a cruise ship heading to Ireland with his mother. Later in life, Paddy would put two and two together that Paddy's parents had divorced, but in the meantime, the trip to Ireland seemed like a grand adventure, which Paddy thoroughly enjoyed. His mother quickly befriended several of the ship's staff, all of whom kept an eye on Paddy as he explored the decks and bowels of the ship, an adventure full of surprise and wonder, a fond memory.

Paddy explored the cruise ship daily, scouting the various compartments throughout the ship, top to bottom, front to back—or bow to stern, as sailors would say. Despite all the exploration, including sneaking out of the cabin at night, he never made it outside, which in hindsight, a six-year-old, especially one who was fearless, outside on a ship's deck would not have been a good idea

WELCOME TO IRELAND

A week on the ship seemed like a forever adventure to Paddy until the blast of the ship's foghorn woke him up early one morning as the ship entered the Port of Galway,  Ireland. A new adventure was ahead. Paddy and his mother waited at the dock with other passengers for the baggage to be offloaded. Eventually, a man in a car arrived and took them on what Paddy thought was a long drive, which in truth was about an hour's drive to arrive at his mother's childhood home in the countryside of Kilkenny.

The car pulled up in front of the house that would be home for the next four years. An excited Paddy jumped out of the car and set out to explore. There was a chill in the air, and it was an overcast day—typical fall weather for Ireland. The first thing that caught his attention and fascination was a dozen or so chickens pecking at the ground by the right side of the house. The one-story small house sat about fifteen feet from the side of a narrow black-top paved road, about the width of a single-lane road. Paddy looked curiously at the roof of the house that seemed peculiar in that the roof was made of straw, known as a thatched roof. The walls of the house were dirty white whitish made of rough stucco. On the right side of the house stood a wooden shed and, next to the shed, the chicken coop. A metal drainpipe ran from the shed's metal roof to a large barrel full of rainwater.

Reacquaintances

Paddy vaguely remembered his mom's family from previous visits. There was Aunt Joe, short for Josephine, a short, dark-haired woman in her forties with black rim glasses who always wore what Paddy would remember as being a dark-colored work apron. There was Aunt Peg, Aunt Joe's sister who dressed like Joe, without the glasses, and had long dark hair that was always rolled up in an updo. Peg had a job at a farm, and every morning would get on her bicycle and pedal to work. Years later, Paddy would learn that Aunt Joe was actually his mom's mother, a secret Paddy never really understood nor cared to investigate.

There was Grandpa Joe, an old man that Paddy remembered wearing a long overcoat, who walked with a wooden cane and wore a tweed flat hat commonly known as a newsboy cap. He smoked a pipe, and when opportunity presented itself, he would blow the smoke in Paddy's face, resulting in a coughing spell and one of the contributing factors for Paddy never taking up smoking as an adult. On numerous occasions, Grandpa would purposely ambush Paddy with loud, obnoxious vomit-inducing burps that forever left an impression and lifelong revulsion to future burps.

Bedpans and Tree Lines

The Ireland of the 1960s was a stark contrast to New York City, although Paddy was not disappointed or even noticed. Well...he probably did notice the absence of running water, a sink, or bathroom, and that the daily bathroom requirements were conducted with a bedpan at night and outside during the day alongside a tree line. The barrel of water he had noticed outside was used for bathwater.

Drinking water was collected from a water pump about a mile down the road, and Paddy would soon learn the task of carrying two buckets to the pump and carrying the buckets of water back to the house, which by final arrival were usually two half- or quarter-buckets of water. His competency in this chore improved over time.

Google Maps shows that the pump is still there – although no longer working

Adjustments

There was one modern amenity in the single light bulb that hung from the ceiling. Electricity was a new luxury in many areas of rural Ireland. A single door at the front of the house led into a large room that had a fireplace to the right and a faded red couch against the wall on the left. On the wall opposite the front door was a small table that served as the kitchen table under a small narrow window that overlooked a garden behind the house. There was another small room behind the fireplace wall that contained three single beds. Later that evening, Paddy would learn that the couch would be his bed.

The adventure of Ireland included meeting new friends and adjusting to understand the Irish accents, a difficult task attempting to understand what on many occasions sounded more like incoherent ramblings instead of rational conversations. Paddy adjusted, quickly learned and adapted to the language and to a new school that required a daily walk on a trek that, years later and with magic of Google, Paddy would discover was a distance of a little over two miles, and as for how long it took to walk the distance, Paddy had no idea, he just walked while accumulating a collection of other children along the way.

First Communion

The first year in Ireland passed without incident or misadventures, his mischievous nature and inclination to do what others may find harmful temporarily in check. All was good, Paddy had friends, attended school, and participated in preparation for the traditional Catholic First Communion. As Paddy remembered it, First Communion was a big deal, and all the children from the surrounding churches received their First Communion together at a ceremony at St Mary's Cathedral in Kilkenny. The girls wore white dresses, and the boys wore a mix of their best clothes. After his First Communion, Paddy became an altar boy.

Paddy learned to play the Irish sport of hurling, a sport Paddy considered similar to the stickball played on the streets of New York City. When not in school, over the summer and on weekends, Paddy explored the countryside. He found a castle that he regularly explored, which again with the magic of Google, he would later learn was a straight distance of just under two miles across farm fields from the house, and sixty years later was restored to a three-bedroom home in 2019. His adventures to the castle were many, and imagination was employed within the dusty, deteriorating castle.

Tubbrid Castle

THE BARN'S ON FIRE

Paddy would recall his mother being a prolific musician, demonstrating her variety of skills on an accordion and fiddle on Friday and Saturday nights at the nearby Butler's Pub. Nearby being a misstatement in that the pub was a few miles away from home, next to that water pump where Paddy would draw buckets of water. On the weekend evenings when his mother was at the pub, so was Paddy. He was a regular, ordering and partaking in a frosty-topped glass of Guinness. The taste of Guiness was distinctive and in ways very similar to the color and foaminess of root beer.

Paddy would go about playing, watching his mother play the accordion and fiddle, and on one occasion, she accompanied four men singing, all dressed in white matching cardigans. Their performance was enjoyed by everyone. Paddy did not know the foursome were a famous Irish quartet, supposedly The Clancy Brothers. The nights at the pub left a lasting impression of his mother's music. The heavy smoke-filled pub caused Paddy's eyes to burn, forcing him to spend much of the time outside and providing another lesson that left a lack of desire to ever smoke.

Paddy learned a lot at the pub, which was also a farm. He learned how to milk cows, drive a tractor, and use a horse-drawn plow, although he never became very good at it. He played outside around the farm and in the hay barn, which to Paddy's eyes and imagination was two stories high.

As a child's mind works and plunders through their fantasies, many children explore the proverbial what do they want to be when they grow up, and Paddy went through a very short-lived period of wanting to be a fireman.

A year after their arrival in Ireland, on a summer evening in 1963, the was sun still up, Paddy was playing in the back of the barn and thought it was a good idea to practice being a fireman by starting small fires that he would put out. Access to match books was unlimited since his mother and most everyone smoked cigarettes. The first few tries of these fire experiments were successful. However, Paddy's limited knowledge of fire science, limited availability of nearby water, and limited knowledge of the flammability of vast quantities of dry hay in a large hay barn perplexed Paddy when he ignited the match and set a tiny straw house he had built on fire. His futile attempt to extinguish the fire of his tiny house was not cooperating.

The fire ignored Paddy's furious demands, slaps, and other efforts to put it out. The fire immediately made its attempt to escape Paddy's control, and it did so without effort. Within seconds, the fire jumped from the tiny house onto an ocean of kindling, thrilled as it observed it was surrounded by a barn filled to the brim with dry hay. It was party time for the fire, as it took full advantage of the conditions while Paddy's continued attempts to vanquish the fire failed. Paddy's initial denial that the fire was out of control lasted only a few seconds as he observed and learned how quickly fire could spread. The fearless Paddy was hit by reality and the heat of the flames as he watched fire quickly spread. The fire was out of control and out of *his* control.

"The barn's on fire! The barn's on fire!" a screaming Paddy yelled as he ran from the barn across the courtyard toward the pub. His yelling caught the attention of the men standing outside the pub, and as he ran, he watched them spring into action. Paddy continued yelling and running toward the pub as the men raced past him to the

barn. Paddy reached the pub front door and was greeted by everyone inside running out the door to go fight the fire.

The group of about twenty or more men were busy putting the fire out, a task that would take hours. Paddy sat quietly on a bench in the entry of the pub, avoiding eye contact with those who passed by him. No one spoke a word as they ignored him, except for the pub's collie dog, who kept Paddy company. His mother sat with him briefly and asked what happened. He was honest and told her that he was playing fireman. Other than a look of amazed disappointment, he was not beaten, scolded, or punished. More psychology was employed by his mother and Paddy knew what he had done.

EVERYTHING CHANGED

A week later, it seemed like the fire had been forgotten, although Paddy would never forget the life lesson he had learned. Paddy's mother had a way about her, as many parents do, in that resorting to a spanking, a beating, verbal abuse, or punishment was not employed and with just a few words followed by her nonverbal manner instilled a lasting lesson about not playing with fire, more so than any punishment would have.

Months later, Paddy was at Butler's Pub with his mother on an early Monday evening. It was odd being at Butler's on a Monday, and to Paddy, it seemed like everyone in the world was there. The pub was filled with people drinking and talking, and many of them took turns to approach Paddy, shaking his hand and telling him, "Sorry about your president."

Paddy didn't understand why they were saying that to him as they watched a small black and white television showing the funeral of President John F. Kennedy.

Earlier in the year, Paddy's mother had married a local man, a coal miner. Paddy remained at Aunt Joe's, and his mother and her new husband lived somewhere else. He saw his mother often, and their weekend evening routine at Butler's Pub continued where his mother played music and he drank his tall glass of imitation Guinness, but now he stayed clear of the barn.

The arrival of spring in 1964 also brought a baby sister. Over the next few months, the baby sister spent most of her time away with their mother until a morning in mid-September when Paddy was getting ready to leave for school and a car arrived with his mother and six-month-old sister. His mother talked to Aunt Joe and then talked with Paddy before giving him a hug and kiss before she got into the car and left. In the moment, it did not register with Paddy that his mother was leaving to return to the United States, leaving him and his sister behind. However, the memory was scorched in his mind for future strategic reference.

Life remained normal, even without the presence of his mother. The eight-year-old Paddy attended school, and his routine of playing and exploring continued and expanded, although now, he also spent time with his sister. He occasionally made new friends with the children from the traveling Tinkers, which was another name for gypsies, who took up their temporary residences along roadways.

The parish priest, Father Mike, ran a boxing club for boys every August through October, and they practiced at the church annex building on Fridays. The small black and white television at home added to the limited home

activity. Imagination ran vividly wild with the once-a-week arrival of The Man from U.N.C.L.E. and a popular British show called The Avengers, for which young Paddy developed his boyish obsession for Emma Peel.

Paddy's mother wrote letters and always sent money in the envelope. During this period, the Butlers had a new modern technological gadget installed at the pub; it was a telephone. The telephone was situated in a makeshift phone booth in a side room away from the pub. An occasional phone call was scheduled in advance in a letter with a set day and time. With the end of that school year in June of 1965, Paddy's explorations grew more extensive and lengthier for the eight-year-old. Aside from his adventures, he was on occasion exposed to various stories of folklore to include Banshees, something which he initially did not believe in, and with the arrival of August, boxing practice began.

THE CANDLE HOUSE

As Paddy remembered it, the weekly boxing practice meetings were held on late Friday afternoons and lasted a few hours into the evening. Boxing practice started in August and lasted through late October, coinciding with seasonal festivals. The two-mile walk to practice usually took about thirty to forty minutes. After practice, the assortment of young boxers played and joked as they left the church annex.

As the summer ended and fall approached, the sun set earlier and the chillier fall weather hastened Paddy's treks home, but not too much as there was always something to explore or imagine. With each passing week, darkness approached faster, until complete nightfall happened by the time Paddy reached home. The dark didn't bother Paddy; remember, he was fearless. The walk home on the first night of near darkness was cloudy with a slight breeze that produced the light sound of wind blowing through the tree line and chest-high dry brush bordering the roadway.

Paddy crested the top of the slight incline of the hill, with home a quarter mile ahead on the right. A flicker of light caught his attention to his left. Paddy stopped and looked at the two-story large house situated about a hundred yards from the road. He curiously took steps past the entry gate on the pathway toward the home, stopping every few steps to focus on the light and avoid the clutter of overgrowth along the way. As he drew closer, he saw the light clearer in a ground-floor window. Paddy took a few more steps, stopped, and studied the house.

Why no lights, why a candle? He thought about it and looked for the power line leading from the road to the house. It was difficult to see, so he made his way back to the electric pole by the road. He was surprised to see there was not a power line. He thought, funny, they don't have electricity. Then he wondered who they were. He didn't see anyone at the table where the candle sat just inside the window. No other candles were lit, just the one. As he thought about it, he never remembered seeing anyone at that house or in the overgrown front yard, and he always assumed it was empty. He ventured back to the house, examining the structure, looking for any other signs of life. From a distance, he peered at each of the eight windows: four on the ground floor and four on the top floor.

An unfamiliar faint sound caught his attention. The night breeze had already been whistling through the trees and bushes with an occasional increase in its howling as overpassing clouds temporarily blocked out the moonlight. With each blast of the wind, Paddy was puzzled by a faint screeching noise. The noise wasn't loud and seemed to blend with the wind, and it seemed to change from a faint short screech to something more like a lingering howl, all of which sparked Paddy's interest. What is that? It sounded like it was the wind, but it also seemed to come from inside the house.

Paddy stood in front of the candle-lit window, taking occasional precautionary glances around him while questioning the logic of a lit candle in a presumedly empty house while deflecting his body's instinct to have a periodic chill from the cold wind. The combination of the chill from the wind and the continued screech and howling induced a heightened sensation of anxiety and curiosity. Paddy's curiosity about the odd noises diminished as they seemed to grow in intensity with each passing gust of wind, and what had been curiosity changed to a feeling of being annoyed, as he felt an unexplained impression that the noise was getting louder and closer.

Unable to make sense of or understand it, Paddy's annoyance grew into frustration. Enough of this, he thought, taking one more glance at the candle. In orchestrated unison, overcast clouds blocked out the moonlight again and a strong gust of wind blew and then completely stopped. In the same moment the wind stopped, the candle flickered, accompanied by a high-pitched screech from the house as the candle became extinguished.

Paddy ran, yelling, "Bloody hell. God, bloody hell!" He tripped, got back up, and kept running until he was on the road. He walked briskly toward home, looking over his shoulder. His mind raced. He could not make sense of what had happened. By the time he was inside at home, he rationalized that it was the wind making noises and that a breeze through the house blew out the candle. It was that simple. The idea or stories of Banshees was not a thought, especially since he had not yet heard about Banshees.

Paddy thought about asking his Aunt Joe and Peg about who lived in the house, but his young mind wanted to avoid getting in trouble for not coming straight home. As he laid in bed, his mind raced with curiosity and imagination about the house and the candle. It was the wind that blew out the candle, right?

The Cat and the Bird

The next day, Saturday, while Paddy was on his adventures, he made his way to the candle house. He stopped by the entry, and like a soldier on a reconnaissance mission, he observed, studied, and made mental notes. He asked himself questions that he tried to answer. Why did it look like no one lived there? The front and side of the house was overgrown with knee-high grass, brushes, and weeds. He built his courage up and cautiously made his way to the front of the house, to the window with the candle. The remains of the candle were there on the old wooden table, the wick just a nub on the table surrounded by a melted layer of candle wax. It looked like it had burned out. Maybe that's what happened. It wasn't the wind; the candle just burned out.

The candle sat on the far end of the table away from the window. There was a chair by the table, pushed away like someone had been sitting in it and had pushed it back to get up. The room Paddy was looking at was the main room of the house. There was another window to the left, and to the right was the door to the house. He peered through the window and saw a fireplace on the left of the room and two smaller windows on the far side of the room. No furniture, only the table and chair by the front window in that giant room.

The curiosity was overpowering, accompanied by a gazillion questions. Paddy moved to the other side of the door and slowly peeked in the first window, a small room with an open entrance to the room on the left. A single-sized bed was by the far side wall and looked neatly made with a blanket covering it, and a wooden chair was positioned next to the foot of bed. A candlestick holder sat on the chair without a candle. Paddy moved to the second window, a look inside another bedroom. This one had the entrance on the far wall, and nothing was in the room.

The temptation was burning as Paddy walked back to the door and stood in front of it, contemplating knocking. He stirred up his courage and knocked, knocked again, and again. With no answer to his knocking, he figured that no one was home and with some hesitation decided to enter what he thought was a giant empty house.

He grabbed the door handle and tried with his thumb to push down on the latch. The latch didn't move. He tried both of his thumbs to push the latch down. As he pushed down on the latch, he heard the metal clang of the latch moving and gently pushed the wooden door inward. The door creaked on its rusted metal hinges. The sound added to Paddy's building anxiety. He pushed the door halfway open and peaked around it. Without warning, Paddy was startled by the screaming hiss of a black cat that jumped off the staircase banister at him, causing him to leap back and fall against the doorframe as the cat scurried around Paddy's feet and ran out the door.

Paddy stepped away from the doorway. The momentary scare gave Paddy pause as he considered canceling his exploration. This pause was cut short by the fluttering of a small bird's wings and its panicked chirping as it left its hidden nest above the doorway within the straw thatched roof.

"Bloody hell again!" Paddy yelled from sudden fright as he stepped further away from the doorway and looked up at a large crow on the roof cawing. He glanced at the windows, still curious as to if someone could be inside but scared enough for the day to run home, leaving the door open.

Paddy's curiosity of the house he referred to as the candle house was soon quenched as there were other explorations to go after, including the nearby castle. Although two miles may not be considered nearby, for Paddy, it was one of his favorite explorations. He explored every inch, room, and floor of the four-story castle and played throughout it, imagining being a king or a knight running around the floors of the castle.

A Lesson About Banshees

A week later, on the next Friday, Paddy went to boxing practice. On his way home, darkness was settling, and it was a breezy evening, overcast, with a quarter moon. Imagination filled Paddy's mind during his travel home. As he approached the candle house, a voice in his head told him to look at the house again, while another voice told him not to. It only took a few seconds for youthful compulsion to take over, and as he passed the entrance to the house, he glanced off to his left and stopped suddenly. A lit candle flickered in the window. His mind filled with conflicting commands. Should I go look in the window again? Paddy thought about investigating, but the voice of reason in his head persuaded him to withdraw and keep heading home.

Paddy kept walking until, a few steps later, he stepped on something on the road. He bent down to see what it was and picked it up. The discovery excited him and made him forget about the candle house. He ran the quarter of a mile home and burst through the door. His Aunts Joe and Peg and Grandpa were sitting by the fire, and he cried out, "Look what I found," showing them with pride a black comb.

Paddy's moment of triumph came to an abrupt and frightening end. The expression on his aunts' faces conveyed that he had done something wrong, although he did not know what it was. Aunt Joe and Peg were angry, very angry, and in hindsight years later, Paddy would recall that they were not just angry, but they were frightened. Grandpa sat in his chair staring at the floor shaking his head as both Aunt Joe and Peg stood up to race toward Paddy. Peg got to him first, angrily snatching the comb out of his hand, and stormed to the front door, opened it, and went outside. Paddy looked on as he watched Peg throw the comb across the road. A visibly shaken Peg went back into the house, slammed the door, and as she walked past Paddy, stopped to glare at him. Paddy was scared and crying. Aunt Joe was also crying as Paddy looked back and forth at Joe and Peg for mercy or an explanation. Peg grabbed Paddy by the shoulders, shook him, and started to yell, "You can never, never do that. You can't, can't!"

Peg was so upset, it was difficult for Paddy to understand her yelling.

"Don't ever do that! Don't ever pick up a Banshee's comb! Don't you know that? You better not have brought death to this house... Don't you know about Banshees?"

Peg glared at Joe as Paddy transitioned to hysterical crying.

"Doesn't he know about the Banshees?" Peg yelled at Joe.

"If he doesn't know, he bloody well should know," Grandpa angrily commented.

Aunt Joe didn't answer, but Paddy knew she was scared. He sensed that all three of them were scared, but he didn't understand why. He had heard mention of the banshee but still had no idea what a Banshee was.

The next morning, the previous night's trauma seemed to be a forgotten bad dream. No one mentioned what had happened, and a regular Saturday morning began. Paddy went out to the chicken coop and collected the eggs. Breakfast was a soft-boiled egg and a piece of buttered toast that he toasted over the fireplace.

After breakfast, Paddy went outside to play, and a short time later his grandpa, smoking his pipe, walked up to him, leaned over, and blew smoke in his face, followed by one of those near-vomit-inducing, boiled egg burps. Paddy resisted the urge to vomit while Grandpa had a good laugh. He then rubbed the back of Paddy's head, pulled him in for a hug, and invited him to sit on the bench.

"Tell me, lad...what do you know about da Banshee?"

"Nothing, Grandpa."

They sat on the bench by the shed, and Grandpa began to educate Paddy on the folklore of the Banshees, all the while smoking his pipe. Paddy listened intently to the story, resisting the occasional gag impulse induced by the smoke emitted from Grandpa's puffing of his pipe. The smoke appeared to be destined and determined to float and hover around Paddy's face, which became an annoyance that forced Paddy to stand a few feet away from Grandpa.

Grandpa smiled and laughed at Paddy and continued to tell him all he knew about the Banshees and why he believed Banshees were real. Grandpa told Paddy several stories about how Banshees appeared as old women, sometimes crying and asking for help to find their comb. He warned Paddy to not be fooled by the Banshee because they could also appear as young women and were usually seen by church graveyards or by the side of the road, and always, always at night. He told Paddy that a Banshee appearance meant that death was nearby, and that was why his aunts had been so upset.

Grandpa explained that nearby death was just part of the story about the Banshees, and if there was a Banshee near, then there was also a Reaper nearby.

"The Grim Reaper!" Grandpa dramatically emphasized, describing the Reaper's appearance as a figure wearing a black robe with a hood that covered its face. He told Paddy that some believe a Reaper's face is of a skeleton, but no one knows for sure., because no one has lived to tell. Others say the hood looks empty, faceless, soulless. At this point, Grandpa abruptly stood up, walked to the shed door, and opened it as he continued to tell the story.

"The Reaper carries a long-handled sickle...just like this one!" he yelled as he yanked a six-foot-tall sickle from the shed, holding it extended in front of him as he walked toward Paddy. Grandpa's exaggerated presentation of the sickle scared Paddy for a moment. Grandpa smiled. He was purposely telling the story in a manner to scare Paddy.

Was it a good idea for Grandpa to tell a child as young as Paddy stories about Banshees and Reapers? Most parents and grandparents would say, surely not, not at all. As for Paddy, learning about Banshees as Grandpa explained it meant that Banshees were real and to be feared. Telling Paddy about Banshees at such a young age may not be considered good parenting, but as Paddy would later reflect, being told about it and knowing about the Banshees saved his life.

This newfound knowledge activated Paddy's imagination and curiosity about Banshees. Remember, Paddy was fearless, even though he'd had a few frights. He was determined, if ever confronted, to not fear the Banshee nor fear the Reaper. His young mind and imagination convinced him that he was fearless and could face anything. After all, he'd been exploring the Irish countryside for two years and felt that he was an experienced explorer, studying the open fields, rivers and streams, abandoned ruins, castles, the local pub, and even befriending the occasional traveling Tinker. If he encountered a Banshee, he'd be ready.

The Following Friday

The next week, the walk home from boxing practice was peaceful. Although it was a chilled evening, it was without wind, and the clear starlit sky showcased an almost half-moon. Paddy loved looking at the stars and letting his imagination run. The lesson about Banshees a week earlier was forgotten as his obsessive focus was watching the weekly episode of The Man from U.N.C.L.E. when he got home. Paddy also loved the weekly episode of The Monkees about an American band that aired on Saturday evenings.

Paddy's imagination worked overtime pretending to be an U.N.C.L.E. agent as he walked home. As he neared home, he passed the house on his left, initially ignoring it while his mind was preoccupied with his fantasies. An unintended glance toward the house caught the flicker of a candle in the window, the same window as before, but this time, Paddy wasn't interested and kept walking. When he arrived home, Aunt Joe and Aunt Peg looked at Paddy with cautious suspicion, which Paddy ignored as he turned on the television.

DEATH DELIVERED

The next week passed as usual, and on the following Friday afternoon, Paddy was busy chasing the chickens, trying to catch one of the hens for his Aunt Joe. After a period of extensive persistence on the chickens' part to escape capture, Paddy finally succeeded in catching the slowest chicken. What happened next, Paddy had seen before on an almost weekly basis. Some weekends a pig's head was on the menu instead of chicken, but this weekend it was chicken. The chicken routine consisted of the catching of the chicken, then Aunt Joe putting the chicken on the chopping block, which was a knee-high block of wood, and killing the chicken with an axe for the Saturday and Sunday meals. Every week, Paddy watched and waited because after killing the chicken came the task of plucking the feathers off the chicken, a task that Paddy did not excel at.

The first time Paddy witnessed his Aunt Joe killing a chicken was a horrifying experience for the young Paddy. He watched Aunt Joe hold the chicken by its legs, place the chicken's head on the chopping block, and use a short-handled axe to lob off its head. The chicken reacted instantly to the severing of its own head. Paddy reacted sadly to the unexpected beheading followed by the violent flapping of the chicken's wings while Aunt Joe kept a tight hold on its feet until the flapping stopped, which usually took about a minute.

On this Friday, the execution of the chicken was near as Aunt Joe mentioned the approach of the milk man five minutes down the road and the necessity to hurry. The milk man made a delivery twice a week. Unlike the stereotypical milk man of the United States who dressed in a white uniform and drove a van, this milk man wore regular clothes and drove a one-horse drawn short cart that carried two silver canisters filled with milk.

As Paddy had witnessed countless times in the past two years, Aunt Joe took the chicken, got a firm hold of its legs, positioned its head on the chopping block, and, with her other hand holding the short-handled axe, swung down. When the chicken's head flew off, what Paddy saw was not an ordinary chicken upset about having its head cut off. No, this chicken reacted differently. This chicken wasn't just upset or angry, it was furious, violently gyrating and flapping its wings. In Paddy's mind, he would swear he heard the chicken cackling the entire time, even though without its head, that was impossible.

With that chop of the axe, the chicken violently flapped, so much so that Aunt Joe struggled to hold on to its legs, even after dropping the axe and using both hands. The chicken violently flapped and squirmed, while Aunt Joe tried her best to hold on as it looked like the chicken was

gaining altitude with every sequence of flaps. Joe's arms were extended up and in front of her, valiantly holding on until the chicken broke Aunt Joe's grasp, flapping its wings and making its escape, taking flight away from Aunt Joe, gaining a slight increase in altitude as it flew across the front of the house before the crash landing.

The chicken, still headless, made a speedy recovery, up on its feet, and picked up its escape pace and ran, ran, ran. Paddy watched with amazement, for the first time seeing a chicken literally running with its head cut off, running, running, running. Later in life, he would recall this moment anytime he heard the saying, "like a chicken with its head cut off."

The chicken ran in no particular direction, without a plan, puzzling Paddy as he wondered how long the chicken would run. His aunt seemed to give up trying to catch it. For Paddy, it seemed to last a couple minutes, and while he felt bad for the chicken, watching the headless chicken running did make him laugh. The chicken finally stopped running, its valiant escape attempt over as its body surrendered and collapsed. The task of plucking the feathers began, and Aunt Joe hurried to finish before the milk man arrived.

The mike man pulled up in front of the house on the far side of the road next to a wooden stand and poured fresh milk into a gallon-size container. It was a regular delivery, and sometimes Aunt Joe chatted with the milk man. Paddy wasn't paying much attention to the conversation, still perplexed with amazement at the headless chicken running, until he heard Aunt Joe tell the milk man, "No need to make your stop at McCullough's up there... You heard?"

Paddy noticed Joe and the milk man look toward the candle house.

"What? What about him?"

"That old codger up and died. He lived alone, and one of the lads seen his door open and went in and found him dead."

"Ea, when that happen?"

"About a fortnight."

"Ea, two weeks ya say?"

"They found him Saturday two weeks ago."

The milk man let out a little laugh. "That be why he hadn't got his milk the last few deliveries... Best I be canceling his deliveries then."

The milk man and Joe laughed a little and continued to talk. Paddy stopped listening and walked away, putting together the timeline in his mind. Two weeks...how could that be? The candle was lit last week. Paddy was right, it was one week ago when he seen the candle for the second time in the window again, but McCullough had been dead a week. Same day, the same night, a Friday, he first seen the candle in the window.

Hearing that when he was drawn to the candle and opened the door to the house two weeks earlier that McCullough had been dead, confused Paddy. Was the man already dead? Or was he still alive and maybe he died when Paddy was there that Friday night? Paddy had a lot of questions. Recalling Grandpa's Banshee stories and more stories his friends told him did not help settle Paddy's thoughts. He wondered if a Banshee was there. It made sense to him that maybe he heard the wailing of a Banshee mixed with the wind, and the comb on the road was a clue, and the next morning his grandpa telling him about Banshees and Reapers on the same morning McCullough was found was eerily confusing.

Paddy made his way inside and didn't know what to make of it other than convincing himself there was a Banshee. Aunt Joe came in and started making Paddy his dinner, a bowl of tapioca with raisins—his favorite. Aunt Peg would be home soon, and it would be time to go to boxing practice.

THE ENCOUNTER

After dinner, Paddy left for boxing practice, and along the way, he glanced at the empty house that McCullough used to live in. His imagination was stirred by the news of McCullough, and the sight of the house catapulted his mind into wild thinking about Banshees and Reapers.

After practice, Paddy would chat with his friends in the annex lot and oftentimes found themselves across the road by the graveyard next to the church until the boxing coach, Father Mike, chased them off. Today, they said goodbye to Father Mike and walked toward the road. Halfway to the road, Paddy stopped suddenly, catching his two friends' attention. They asked him what he was doing then noticed him looking at a figure, who appeared to be a woman, standing at the edge of the graveyard.

The sight was strange, an unusual occurrence as there was never anyone there. The sight did not preclude Paddy's friends from making jokes. The woman was turned away from the boys and wearing a long, dark grey coat, and her head was covered with a bright multicolored scarf. As Paddy's friends joked, he remembered what his grandpa had told him about Banshees being seen near graveyards but only at night.

Paddy observed that it was not night yet, although it was close, before dusk, twilight with a shimmer of faded sunlight forcing its way through the clouds and trees. The brisk fall breeze and cloudy sky added to Paddy's apprehensions. His friends detected Paddy's resistance to walking past the woman. They offered, jokingly, to walk with him. The friends usually walked in the other direction to their homes, and Paddy walked alone, past where the woman stood.

As they walked toward the woman, the friends continued to tease Paddy about being afraid of a woman. Upon hearing their jokes, the figure turned around and removed her scarf in a dramatic fashion, stopping the boys in their tracks as her pale face and fiery red hair were revealed.

"Nothing to be afraid of, boys," the green-eyed young woman said in a soft-spoken voice and half smile that gave the friends the creeps and compelled them to say a very quick bye to Paddy, turn, and sheepishly run away. Paddy stood frozen, his mind rapidly contemplating the scenario. *Who is she? She can't be a Banshee. It's too early...isn't it?*

"Don't be afraid, Paddy. I'm not here to hurt you," the woman kindly told Paddy.

"How do you know my name?" he fearfully asked, slowly stepping backwards.

"It's alright, Paddy," the woman reassuringly told him as she extended her hand as if to pat his shoulder.

Panic overtook Paddy, and he backed away then made a dash around the woman toward home. A few seconds later, he slowed to a walk and heard the woman calling out.

"Don't be afraid, Paddy! Be brave and be a strong young lad."

He looked back as he continued to walk, watching the woman put her scarf back on as she took a step in his direction. He quickened his pace, kept watch over his shoulder at the woman, who was still walking in his direction. However, the next time he looked, she was gone. He glanced back a few more times to confirm that the woman was gone, his last glace coinciding with a strong breeze and a realization that it was night.

The encounter with the woman and brisk breeze gave Paddy an uneasy feeling as he walked. He continued to look for the woman and analyze what had happened while he maintained a fast pace.

"Those chickens..." he said out loud with a laugh as he thought about his friends getting scared and running away. Paddy was filled with questions. He wondered how the woman knew his name and who she was. He thought about how his friends turned instantly scared of her once she revealed her hair. He had seen it on their faces...they were terrified. But not him...he was brave, fearless. He was only scared when she said his name and reached for him. He found it odd. What terrified them so much but not him?

Paddy kept asking himself questions about the encounter until about halfway home when the wind picked up and it started to rain. The rain was light, almost misty, but just enough to be miserable. The wind increased, and what made it worse was the wind was blowing into him. The rain turned cold and combined with repeated cold, strong gusts of wind. Paddy found it bothersome walking into the wind and rain and turned his back to the wind and tried walking backwards. Walking backwards only worked for a few steps, and Paddy began a routine of walking into the wind and turning around to walk backward a few steps. A few minutes later, Paddy concluded that his attempts at walking backward were futile and faced into the rainy wind, head down, looking at the ground as he pushed forward, shivering and cursing to himself with each gust of wind.

Paddy marched ahead, only occasionally glancing up from the ground. Nearing the crest of the hill by the candle house, Paddy quickly peeked up to see the house ahead on the left. He looked down and kept marching, determined to get home out of the weather. The gusts of wind continued, however with less intensity, which Paddy noticed as he expressed a sigh of relief. The howling of the wind made varying sounds through the trees and bushes lining the sides of the road, nothing unusual, as the clouds moved swiftly overhead. A sudden break in the clouds exposed a glimmer of moonlight, which filled Paddy with another sigh of relief as he realized he was almost home.

Paddy's spirits picked up as he increased his pace, anticipating his arrival home and sitting in front of the fireplace to dry out and warm up. The rain gradually stopped, and the wind gusts slowed to a breeze. The previous strong howling sounds of the wind diminished to a lower, quieter whisper through the bushes, a welcome change for Paddy as he approached the gateway of the candle house, which by this point, did not distract him nor rekindle previous memories of the house, stories of Banshees, or his encounter with the woman at the graveyard. His only concern was getting home and drying out.

Paddy was set on getting home and picked up his pace again, leaning forward, looking at the ground. The intermittent breezes continued, accompanied by the low whistling and howling of wind through the bushes and the rain started again. He paid no attention to the normal sounds created by the breeze. He looked up and was surprised to see he was in a thick mist, the road ahead was no longer visible, and a thick blanket of fog seemed to rise up to his chest. Although the fog was odd, nothing else about the weather seemed odd or unusual until he glanced at the candle house and stopped. Was that a flicker of light that appeared dimly through the mist from the window? Paddy wasn't sure, but his attention switched to a brief sound of what could be a far-off cry. He ignored it and started to walk again. He didn't think much of the noise and continued on, but then, there it was again—a cry, or moan, or what he thought sounded like an old woman's voice saying something. The odd sound did not slow him down; it was time to speed it up.

Paddy's focus on getting home was abruptly distracted, although briefly, by the stories about the Banshees. Still, he didn't slow down, he didn't look up, he just sped up, trying to ignore the sudden gush of Banshee stories circling in his mind like debris in a tornado. Looking at the ground, he passed the spot of the road where he had found the comb weeks earlier.

"Young boy!" A loud scratchy voice pierced through the fog, overlaid by the breeze.

The creepy voice sounded before a now-terrified Paddy. He stopped and looked up. The tornado in his mind stopped, and his focus changed gears.

"My God!" Paddy screamed, "Bloody hell!" Fearful, Paddy instinctively stepped back, away from an old woman with long grey hair, a sinister smile projecting from her greyish, pale face.

"Have you got my comb, young boy?" the woman asking tearfully, crying through her smile.

Paddy's fear grew as he took another step back and thought, *A Banshee, a real banshee?*

The Banshee lunged at Paddy, her arms reaching for him like branches extending from a tree.

"Give me my comb! Give me my comb!"

Paddy leaped and started to fall backward. The Banshee stopped his fall with both of her hands, grabbed him by the coat collar, and pulled him in close, inches from her face. Paddy went from terrified to bloody terrified ten times over, trying to push the Banshee off.

"Give me my bloody comb, boy!" the Banshee screamed repeatedly at Paddy as he tried to fight the Banshee off.

The banshee had no intention of releasing her grip of Paddy's coat collar. He kept fighting, kicking and screaming, "let me go, let me go," as the Banshee kept demanding her comb. At eye level, the Banshee glared at him. Paddy stopped fighting. He had a sudden feeling that his feet were off the ground. She was holding him, but to Paddy it did not feel like someone had a hold of him anymore. He sensed he was floating, off the ground and face-to-face with the Banshee.

Paddy was frozen with terror. The Banshee released one of her hands and slowly raised it up from his collar toward his face and in a soft, enticing voice commanded, "Give me my comb, boy, give me my comb, and I won't take you."

Paddy did not answer. *Take me where?* he thought. He was paralyzed as he watched the banshee's face transition from a smile to a grotesque expression growing angrier with every second.

"Give me my comb!" she demanded, holding him up above her with one arm. She lowered him back down to eye level and repeated over and over, "Give me my comb." The Banshee raised her hand to Paddy's face and with her index finger tapped his nose. She looked him in the eye and twirled her index finger around his face.

"Boy, it's your choice. If you're not gonna give me my comb, I guess you're going to come with—"

The Banshee's demand was interrupted by a shrill screech that deafened Paddy as he felt himself fall to the ground, flat on his back.

"Leave him be, Banshee! Leave him be!" A deep female voice screamed at the Banshee from behind Paddy.

Lying on his back, Paddy looked up behind him to see a figure yelling at the Banshee. The screeching was so deafening it was difficult for Paddy to decipher what was happening, but within seconds, he recognized the screeching figure as the woman from the graveyard, but there was something different about her. She still had fiery red hair, but instead of flowing behind her, the hair seemed to have a red glow extending from her head. The more she yelled at the Banshee, the more it glowed and intensified in brightness, creating an almost halo effect brightening around her head, and with every angry word she screeched at the Banshee, the brightness expanded down her body toward Paddy. The screeching and approaching light scared Paddy more than the Banshee did.

Paddy convinced himself that it was time to overcome his paralysis, to be brave, to be fearless, so he began a slow backward crawl while he watched the glowing woman and Banshee argue. It was as if they were arguing over his soul.

As Paddy backed away, the arguing continued. From the ground looking up, he thought the terrifying Banshee was not so terrifying anymore and seemed to be afraid of the glowing woman.

Paddy found it difficult to stand up and kept slowly crawling away until he froze when the banshee looked at him with a sneer and pointed her finger at him. The glowing woman glanced toward Paddy. Her face was different than earlier. She snarled angrily at him.

"Go home, Paddy! Go home!"

Paddy didn't move, frozen as he stared at her for a moment...a moment too long. The woman screeched at him, "Go home, go home!" as a burst of light emitted from the woman.

Paddy stumbled backward, like a sand-locked crab running for the water, until he finally made it to his feet, stumbling to a stop as he faced the candle house, where, for one of his common brief yet lingering moments that Paddy indulged in, he looked in disbelief at the entryway of the candle house... "A Reaper!" he blurted out.

"Go home!" the deafening screech from the woman lashed out again.

Paddy turned, and he noticed that the fog was gone. "Go home!" Paddy ran. He ran for his life. Recalling a fox hunt he had seen, he knew he had to run faster than the hare. Fearful curiosity kept him looking over his shoulder at the woman and the Banshee. The fog was gone, but the earlier rain had left a misty effect in the air as the illumination from the woman dimmed. It took a minute of running to get home, and when he reached the front of the house, he was overwhelmed with a sense of diminishing fear, exhaustion, and trouble breathing combined with an unlikely exhilaration. Paddy bent over, hands on his knees, his asthma flaring up as he peered through the mist at the glow of the woman for a few more seconds, and then another loud screech coincided with the glow vanishing.

While Paddy stood bent over gasping for air and contemplating going inside, he kept an eye up the road with no sight of the woman or Banshee. However, as a few seconds passed and his vision focused, something or someone appeared in the road but, it was difficult to make out,. A brief break in the cloud-covered sky exposed the figure for a few seconds. "The Reaper!" Paddy told himself with a shiver. The figure looked very much like the Reaper, complete with its sickle.

The sight of a Reaper deployed additional anxiety in Paddy's heart that increased his shortness of breath. Wheezing, he kept his eye on the reaper that stood motionless in the road. *Was it really a Reaper?* he questioned, but continued to convince himself that it was a Reaper. And then it hit him—a sudden, overwhelming feeling of depression, remembering the part of the Banshee stories about approaching death.

McCullough died the night Paddy thought he might have heard the Banshee the first time. He grew worried, concerned about why the Banshee was there. *And why the Reaper?* Paddy's concern increased his anxiety as he tried to stand straight up, gasping, wheezing. *Were they here for Grandpa, or...for me?*

The door of the house opened, and his Aunt Joe walked out yelling at him.

"Jesus, Paddy! What are you doing? Get in here out of the cold, it'll be the death of you."

Paddy didn't move, he couldn't move. The asthma had him, and Aunt Joe recognized it. She walked him inside the house and sat the shivering Paddy down by the fire. She fetched a shot glass filled with Irish whiskey to quell his asthma. The whiskey was only used as a remedy when the asthma attacks were extreme. Paddy drank the whiskey and enjoyed the warmth it gave him in his stomach. He sat close, very close, to the fire and watched the steam rise from his trousers.

Paddy was exhausted and filled with confusion and questions. He sat by the fire for half an hour, wheezing and drying out. Imagination and rationalization went to battle in his young, perhaps delusional, mind, providing a variety of explanations, some outlandish, some doomful, and others a start of the well-known practice of repression.

The Asthma

The night of seeing the Banshee, the reaper, and the woman who glowed was not the first time Paddy had had an asthma attack. His first year in Ireland was uneventful health wise, a few sniffles, but as the second winter approached, troubles breathing crept up. A doctor might say that a damp climate was the culprit that brought on the asthma.

During his second year in Ireland, asthma was diagnosed and a few experimental remedies were tested with injections, an inhaler, and vitamins, all of which were priced beyond the financial resources available, and even a visit to the big Catholic church in Kilkenny to pay the priest for prayers were not affordable except for the one time and, like the medical remedies, did not work to relieve Paddy's asthma. The asthma was another reason Paddy grew up to not become a cigarette smoker as he learned to have a very special appreciation for air. There was one time when Paddy was on his death bed...wait, that night hasn't happened yet.

After the Encounter

When the next morning arrived, it was as if nothing had happened the night before, not even the asthma. Paddy was refreshed and up for breakfast: toast with orange marmalade, a soft-boiled egg, and fresh orange juice. He was extra excited because he would be heading out to the church annex to meet his boxing cohorts and be picked up by Father Mike to head to the fairgrounds where they would participate in boxing matches.

Later that night, as Paddy was working on falling sleep, he thought about the fun he had at the fair. His thoughts drifted to the encounter the previous evening. A day later, reflecting on the fear experienced by the triple encounter with not just the Banshee but the Reaper and the redheaded woman, it was the woman that he could not make any sense of. *Was she another Banshee competing for his soul? Was she a ghost, or could she be an angel, a Guardian Angel?*

Too many questions filled his mind, and as the frightening moments continued to pop up, Paddy attempted to rationalize what had happened. The psychological tactic of repression was in its infancy, but with each flashback of the encounter, repression exercises repeated, and within days, the events of that night were a distant memory—not even a memory, a repressed memory.

By Sunday morning, Paddy's repression exercise was set in place. He no longer had a bad memory, not even a worry in the world, as he set out to church and his altar boy duties. After church, Sunday chicken dinner, and some exploring, he was back to school Monday and the rest of the week, savoring bread and butter sandwiches for lunch.

DEATH FROM ABOVE

Friday morning, Paddy headed off to school as usual. The school day was like many others, and the near hour walk home started as usual. The early part of the walk usually included about twenty to thirty children of varying ages. The group thinned out along the way. Halfway along the walk, curiosity was sparked by a distant repetitive caw, caw, caw of some crows up ahead. The pace quickened to investigate. Within minutes, they approached a couple of work trucks in the roadway and heard the buzz of chainsaws. The sound of crows cawing was loud. Men were working on a cut-down tree, cutting it into smaller pieces. Four other men with chainsaws were working on cutting down another large tree nearby. The sounds of several chainsaws blending with the cawing of hundreds, or even thousands of crows was too loud for the young ears.

Two of the men stepped onto the road and yelled out for the children to move back. Excitement and anticipation grew as the large tree was on the verge of falling. As Paddy and the other children waited, watched, and cheered, the tree began to sway as chainsaws continued to buzz.

"All rights, lads, back," one of the men yelled when the chainsaws stopped. It didn't take long for the tree to sway in one direction away from the road, toward the field on the other side of the tree line. The crackling and breaking of branches began, joined by the yells and cheers of the children and the increasing intensity of the cawing crows.

The tree began its fall, the cawing of the crows intensified, accompanied by the crackling of wood as the tree took only seconds to hit the ground. As the tree fell, a blanket of crows flew out of the tree, attempting their escape. To Paddy's eyes, there were thousands of crows, enough to darken the sky above and cause many of the children to duck and run to avoid the onslaught of the squadron of birds.

The tree safely on the ground, the children yelled in excitement and ran to the tree. Paddy hesitantly followed while the blanket of crows flew away into the distance. Although the crows flew away, the sound of what seemed like hundreds of crows still cawing and screeching remained. As Paddy neared the downed tree, he observed most of the other children jumping up and down, yelling, grabbing branches, thrashing and stomping on the tree, its branches, and the ground with their feet and other branches. Paddy was perplexed by the other children's actions. At first he found it amusing, but he didn't understand what they were doing and why they seemed so happy doing it.

A few of the other children abruptly turned and walked away from the tree, verbally expressing disapproval and visibly upset at what they had witnessed. As Paddy approached, he was distracted by a noise on the ground. He stopped and glanced down at a large injured and dying black crow flapping its wings and cawing. The sight disturbed Paddy, initiating a sense of sadness as he instinctively knelt down to help, touching the chest of the bird. The bird slowly flapped its wings, and the changing colors caught Paddy's attention. Each flap of the wings seemed to change their color from black to shades of blue, green, and purple—an odd sight, to say the least.

Paddy studied the bird.
"I'm sorry."

A tear fell from Paddy's eye as he looked up and suddenly understood what the other children were doing by their thrashing, beating, and stomping. They were killing the crows...hundreds of them.

Paddy stood, saying "I'm sorry" again to the bird, but childish curiosity compelled him to take a closer look, a mistake he immediately regretted. He was repulsed by the images of dead and dying crows, battered by the other children. The loud cries of the injured crows seemed endless as Paddy ran to the road and distanced himself from the field of dying crows and continued his walk home, a walk that would take another half hour.

During his walk, he experienced something he had never felt before. Paddy had never seen anything killed or even dead before...well, except for those chickens...but this felt different. A feeling of grief and sadness struck him, while his stomach tightened and he almost gagged. The feeling returned endlessly during his walk, and a headache hit Paddy unlike any he had ever had. He tried desperately to forget the sight of the dead and dying crows and even found himself crying at times at what now had become an annoying sound of crows cawing repeatedly.

Paddy's hurried pace to get home slowed when he passed Butler's Pub and the water pump. He stopped at the pump for a few minutes, drank some water, and restarted the walk. He wanted to forget about the crows and launched his imagination to the alternating fantasies of being an U.N.C.L.E. agent and singing Monkees' songs in his head—a tactic that seemed to work, at least temporarily.

Upon arriving home, the traumatization of the crows was still on his mind, compounded by a pair of large crows landing on the roof and letting out a double caw. At the time, Paddy didn't know the difference between a crow and the larger, but similar in appearance, raven, the same type of bird he had knelt by. Paddy watched the ravens until Aunt Joe walked out and greeted Paddy as she headed to the chicken coop.

"Where's Grandpa?"

"He's out and about, out and about."

A caw from the rooftop coincided with the answer and distracted them. Paddy went about helping Aunt Joe catch a chicken. As usual on Fridays, the task of catching, killing, and plucking the chicken feathers was completed, as was the milk delivery. The rest of the late afternoon passed, and Paddy had his tapioca with raisins for dinner and then left for boxing practice.

GRANDPA'S CANE

The 1965 season's last boxing practice concluded at the church annex. The boys were excited and looking forward to tomorrow's trip to the fairgrounds and their final boxing match. As they had done after every practice, some of the boys played outside in the annex parking lot and across the street at the church graveyard until Father Mike sent them on their way.

This year there was a new boy, Shamus, who walked the same way with Paddy. The boys departed, and on queue, two ravens that perched on the same gravestone every week departed when Paddy and Shamus did. It turned out that two boys walked slower and explored longer than one boy, and Paddy's arrival home tended to be later. Shamus walked with Paddy until a fork in the road, five minutes before the candle house.

The dusk to dark transition occurred as Paddy and Shamus approached the fork in the road and the boys parted ways. Paddy continued to head home without hesitation or a thought of the previous week's repressed encounter nor the field of dying crows from earlier this afternoon.

Paddy's imagination jumped into full Man from U.N.C.L.E. mode with a special guest appearance by Emma Peel (remember, that boyish crush). He unintentionally glanced at the candle house and was pleasantly surprised at the absence of a lit candle. Unlike the previous week, there was a clear sky and the moon shone from his left over the horizon.

A short minute after the candle house, Paddy looked ahead and saw someone standing in the road in front of the house. At first he didn't recognize who it was until the person started walking toward him. The bright moon illuminated Grandpa. Paddy recognized his walk, hat, and long coat he always wore. Paddy was ecstatic to see Grandpa and sped up his pace. As they got closer to each other, Paddy noticed something.

"Where's your cane, Grandpa?"

They continued to walk toward each other, but Grandpa did not answer.

"Grandpa, did you hear me? Where's your cane?"

Paddy was not concerned...it was Grandpa, the spitting image of him, and Paddy assumed Grandpa couldn't hear him. A few seconds later, Paddy noticed something else. Grandpa usually walked with a limp, which was one of the reasons he used a cane, but Paddy saw that Grandpa, wasn't limping.

"Grandpa...where's your cane?"

A few steps from each other, Grandpa extended his arms, reaching for Paddy as if for a hug, something that Grandpa never did.

"Grandpa?"

Paddy stopped, suspicious, and slowly stepped backward.

"Grandpa?"

Paddy kept moving backward, a move that exposed the appearance of the Reaper behind Grandpa. Terror hit Paddy, and he yelled, "Grandpa, look out, there's a Reaper behind you!"

Grandpa increased his reach for Paddy, the arms stretching out from under the coat sleeves as he spoke in a scratchy old woman's voice. "We've already got your grandpa... Time for you to join him, Paddy."

Right in front of his eyes, the grandpa he knew transformed, morphing into the Banshee, her arms exaggeratedly stretching out for Paddy, her face changing to the grotesque face he remembered.

"Come here, boy... I got you now."

Paddy fell back to the ground and cried out.

"No, no, no, not this time, nope."

When he hit the ground, Paddy didn't hesitate, immediately leaping to his feet, out of reach of the Banshee, and ran into the tree line to his right, the same side of the road as his house. With the Banshee yelling and screeching for him, he ran through the bushes into the field and made a left turn toward home. It was a short run, just a minute to the tree line that bordered the house and through the bushes, out to the space by the chicken coop, and one more dart to the door.

He flew through the door, and as he turned to close it, the screech of the Banshee was heard, startling Aunt Joe, Peg, and a few visitors. They nervously prattled on about the screech. As Paddy closed the door, he thought he saw something resembling a Reaper across the road in the shadows. He quickly closed the door and turned. No one said anything to him, as if Paddy wasn't there, but Aunt Joe did notice him, and from his expression, she knew that something was wrong. Paddy looked by the fireplace and there it was...Grandpa's cane at its spot where Grandpa set it when he sat by the fire, but Grandpa wasn't there.

Aunt Joe, a tear in her eye, watched Paddy, unnoticed by the half dozen visitors as he weaved between them to the fireplace. He grabbed the cane and took it with him to a corner of the couch and sat down. Aunt Joe followed, sat with him, and gave him a hug. Words were not said. The Banshee had already told Paddy that his grandpa was gone, and the look on Paddy's face along with the symbolism of him grabbing the cane told Aunt Joe that Paddy somehow knew.

Paddy watched and listened to the visitors and was aware of Aunt Joe's and Peg's somber moods. He knew that Grandpa must have died before he left for school that morning. He remembered that when he arrived home after school, the traumatization of the crows overshadowed the unusual absence of Grandpa and the unusual presence of visitors. Other than the occasional pipe smoke blown in his face and abrupt burps, Paddy had grown fond of Grandpa, more so after the education lesson about Banshees. During the rest of the evening, there was no mention of the passing of Grandpa.

THE CALM BEFORE

Grandpa was buried within the week, and Paddy had the honor of being an altar boy for the service. Paddy's mother returned for a short visit from the States, but as she had previously done, on a school morning, she gave Paddy a hug and goodbye kiss before leaving again in a car. This time it registered with Paddy what was happening, a situation he attempted to take advantage of, settling for a promise from his mother to send a package from the United States with gifts. Paddy and his sister were left again.

Life continued for Paddy, school continued, and an occasional letter and that package from his mother arrived in time for Christmas. Winter and spring passed, and the approach of summer of 1966 created anticipation for the end of the school year and the longer days to be filled with adventures and explorations. Everything was calm and peaceful for Paddy. During TV time, he immersed his imagination with the Monkees, the Man from U.N.C.L.E., Avengers, and a new British show about Robin Hood.

Paddy's interest in watching what seemed to be an always present couple of ravens no longer stirred the bad memories of the dead crows; he had the practice of repression in full lockdown. Paddy's interest in the ravens had progressed to a relationship, more like pets, in which Paddy found himself talking with them and imagined that they were talking to him, always making him aware of their presence with a caw.

The onset of summer filled Paddy's days with helping Aunt Joe watch after his sister and fetching buckets of water from the pump by Butler's Pub. They also made a trip to Kilkenny to have a picture taken. Paddy played hurling and soccer and went on his adventures throughout the countryside and the old castle. He worked odd jobs with other children for local farmers, sometimes tilling rows of cabbage, which he did not like since it called for hours on his hands and knees pulling weeds. He helped with horses, milking cows, and other farm work. The father of one of Paddy's friends was in the Irish Army and took a liking to Paddy, giving him an army jacket and beret, which may have been his introduction to soldiering and his endless hours playing army.

The beginning of August meant boxing season, an activity Paddy looked forward to and loved, despite the repressed memory of the walks home and his banshee encounters. The previous year's routine of boxing practice once a week and a few travels to carnivals for boxing matches over late summer into fall returned without incident or even a bad or repressed memory of Banshees, reapers, or glowing redheads. All was fine.

NEAR DEATH

This year was just like last year. The last practice of the season was on a Friday evening, and a trip to the carnival was planned for the next day. Paddy began his walk home, and just as it had been the previous year on the final night of practice, the weather was breezy, overcast, with a chill in the air. Playing in the church grounds was broken up as usual by Father Mike, and the boys moved to the road to head home. As Paddy and Shamus approached the road, Paddy unintentionally glanced toward the edge of the graveyard as two cawing ravens departed from atop a headstone. The flying ravens caused Paddy to pause as a memory flashed of the woman by the graveyard. Shamus turned to Paddy, noticing his hesitation.

"What's wrong?"

"Nothin," came Paddy's short reply.

They kept walking, but it wasn't nothing. Paddy experienced a resurgence of the repressed memory attempting to reenter Paddy's mind. He tried resisting, although the woman kept popping up. The two ravens flying overhead and down the road interrupted his thoughts.

"That's bloody weird," Shamus commented as he slapped a pebble on the road with a stick. The boys continued forward, although Paddy tended to get sidetracked with the urgency to get home. Urgency aside, the boys allowed their imaginations to get the best of them, and they played as they went. The overhead clouds gradually darkened, and the breeze changed to gusts of wind, bringing with it a misty rain and the evening twilight. The steady increase in the wind and chill in the air prompted the boys to speed up. When they reached the fork in the road, darkness fell. Shamus headed his way and Paddy, with a feeling of doubt, hesitantly went his way.

Paddy's mind bounced with the familiarity of the year past and how it seemed as if time was repeating itself. The rain wind and its ferocity was the same as that night a year ago, except it was a heavier rain, and Paddy was soon drenched. The intensity of the rain forced him to look down as he tried his best to speed home. The wind blew, its howling effects echoing in the rain. Misery overtook Paddy. He desperately wanted out of the rain. Shivering and wheezing, Paddy glanced ahead with every few steps and was stung by the freezing rain hitting his face.

Paddy pushed ahead, cursing out loud in anger at the wind and rain. His mind was no longer recounting the events of that night a year ago. His only thoughts were about his current misery and how he had never experienced anything like this in his short, young life. He pushed on and decided he would try to run. Paddy glanced up to see where he was. The candle house was to his left, and a sense of triumph hit Paddy, knowing that if he ran and the wind slowed, he could be home in a few minutes. Even if the wind didn't stop, he was close enough now, almost home, and ignored the stinging rain hitting his face, his shivers, his sloshing feet in his shoes, and his wet face and body. He was miserable but determined.

Let's go! he told himself, timing the intervals of the wind as a gust passed. Head down and to the wind, he took his first steps at a run. His wet feet flopped and sloshed on the road.

The caw, caw, caw, caw of the ravens called out through the howling wind, which gave Paddy a fright. He looked up. It was too dark to see any birds flying, but he assumed the cawing was from the ravens. The apparently distressed caw, caw, cawing continued. Paddy shifted his attention from looking for the ravens to the road ahead.

"I still want my comb back, Paddy!" the screaming Banshee yelled out, standing in the middle of the road and lunging for Paddy. He staggered to a stop, slipped, and almost fell, just out of reach of the Banshee. He nervously backed away, staying out of the Banshee's reach while surveying for an escape route. Paddy maneuvered toward the side of the road in hopes that he could go around the Banshee. The intensity of cawing from above increased, like it was getting closer, and combined with the fluttering of wings to distract the Banshee. Paddy made his move around the Banshee while also fighting his increasing difficulty in breathing. He kept his eye on the Banshee, again attempting to lunge after him while erratically waving her arms in the air at the flapping of wings and cawing above her.

Paddy ran, he ran as fast as he could, but his excessive wheezing slowed him down. Every step was frustratingly painful and combined with his panic and fear of the Banshee. The wheezing forced Paddy to stop, only halfway to home. Hands on his knees, he looked back at the Banshee, who was still waving her arms in the air. The sound of the cawing seemed more distant but still intense. Paddy stood and took a step toward home. A minute later, a sudden loud screech from behind Paddy frightened him. He had to stop again and bend over, focusing on the ground, too physically exhausted and scared to move or look behind him.

After a few seconds passed, he didn't hear the ravens anymore. He cautiously looked up and saw the banshee was gone. He stood up, trying to control his wheezing as he began the slow walk to his house. The familiar feeling of not being able to breathe was frustrating and miserable. A few prayers accompanied his frustration, and he wondered about the ravens that had become his friends, Did the ravens save me? Were they somehow protecting me? What about that glowing woman...where was she? Or maybe... The questions loomed and puzzled Paddy as his wheezing grew worse.

The Pneumonia

Paddy made his way to the door, his feet dragging and his wheezing exacerbating. When he entered, Aunts Joe and Peg heard his wheezing, and before he closed the door, they were by his side. They rushed him to the fireplace, and unlike the year before when he sat by the fire to dry off, they stripped the shivering Paddy down, dried him, put dry clothes on him, and wrapped him in blankets. Aunt Joe fetched the shot glass and gave Paddy a drink of that Irish whiskey that warmed his stomach. Joe and Peg were seriously concerned. They dragged the couch that served as Paddy's bed from the far wall twenty feet closer to the fireplace and tucked Paddy in bed.

The shivers did not stop. Early the next morning, Joe and Peg's concern grew when they discovered Paddy still had the shivers, was wheezing, and had a fever accompanied by a cough. Peg jumped on her bicycle and made the trip to Butler's Pub to use the only phone in the area to call for a doctor. The doctor arrived in the afternoon and diagnosed Paddy with pneumonia, a bad combination with asthma. He gave a somewhat delusional Paddy an injection of something and left a bottle of cough medicine and told them he'd visit every day. The days turned into a week with no signs of improvement except for an occasional break from the shivers.

Voices and Visitors

Although there were moments of delusion, or imagination for Paddy, he did have vivid recollection of his bedridden days with the pneumonia of alternating hours of severe decline followed by progress and decline again. The periods of decline were more frequent as days passed, causing concerns. After three or four days, Paddy noticed an increased steady stream of visitors, some in the afternoons and more in the early evenings and observed the visitors looking at him with sorrow on their faces, which was not comforting. He'd observe gatherings and conversations around the fire, and Aunt Joe and Peg brewing batches of tea and serving food that many of the visitors brought with them. It became a daily routine that restarted day after day. The visits became an annoyance to Paddy and felt more like a wake than a friendly visit. It was as if they were waiting for Paddy to die.

Friday afternoon, now a week after that rainy night encountering the Banshee, the doctor paid another visit, without good news. From what Paddy could observe and overhear, his words to Aunt Joe did not appear to be positive and portrayed a sense of hopelessness. As the doctor left, Joe was clearly upset, bringing her to tears. Paddy continued his illness routine of falling asleep and waking up during the day, observing a few visitors and a darkened stormy sky through the front window.

Paddy was woken up by an onslaught of conversations. He opened his eyes and saw visitors, more visitors than he had ever seen before around the house, drinking their tea and whiskey. He heard the faint sound of a fiddle and looked around to see a man sitting at the table playing a fiddle. The entire scene was odd, and with a clap of thunder outside, a nonimaginative revelation hit Paddy. *Bloody hell, God! They're bloody waiting for me to die. I'm not dying, God, am I?* Paddy let out a snicker at his thought, which caught the attention of his friend Shamus standing with a few other friends nearby. Shamus looked at a shivering, feverish Paddy and sat down on the couch next to him. Shamus gave Paddy a smile and a caring tap on the head.

"It'll be fine, Paddy, you'll be fine. They're saying it won't be long now."

"What won't?"

"You'll be dead, and then you'll be fine."

Paddy did not appreciate Shamus's words and honesty. It upset Paddy, and he angrily told Shamus to get out, but given his weakened condition, Shamus did not understand the mumblings Paddy had uttered. Paddy curled up and covered his head with the blankets, shutting out the window and the noise of the room. With his eyes closed and darkness under the covers, his mind raced, and he prayed while blocking out the noise of the conversations and the more frequent thunderclaps. As he prayed, the conversations continued, an occasional laugh was heard, and the creaking of the door opening and closing as visitors came and left.

Paddy stubbornly laid under the covers, practicing the art of intently listening, and learned a lot about the locals.

He found what people talked about when they thought no one else was listening interesting, a life lesson he'd recall later in life.

The Last Rights

"Father Mike's here!" a voice yelled out, followed by grumblings from the visitors. Father Mike! Why is Father Mike here? Paddy grew nervous, not understanding why the priest was there. His nervousness and anxiety exploded when he heard Father Mike's voice introducing Bishop Flynn. A bishop? Why's there a bishop here?

Paddy recalled rumors that priests didn't make house calls except to visit the dead. The menagerie of thoughts running around Paddy's head created doubts and an array of possibilities, but why a bishop? Paddy wondered, Am I dead? A bishop, am I double dead? The conversations continued outside the darkness and confines of the blankets. He was too scared to peek out and burrowed down, determined to stay hidden under the blankets. If he stayed hidden, the priest and that bishop couldn't do whatever it was that they did with the dead.

Paddy heard the door open and what sounded like the visitors leaving. The exodus took some time. The door opened and closed several times, and with every opening, Paddy heard the howling of the wind outside and felt cold enter the room, even under the blankets. Occasionally, Aunt Joe would yell, "Close the bloody door."

Eventually there appeared to be silence outside the blankets. Paddy's curiosity began to spark, interrupted by bouts of shivering and a wheeze. He wondered if he was already dead. That would explain why he couldn't hear anyone. As his mind raced, he worked on building up his courage to peek outside the protective cover of the blankets. He procrastinated, reviewing his options. He heard something that sounded like wood dragging across the concrete flood. The sound stopped, leaving nothing but whispers as Paddy contemplated, trying his best to fight off those shivers.

"Paddy…lad…are you in there?" The voice sounded like Father Mike.

Paddy was conflicted. Scenarios abruptly popped up, asking if Father Mike was dead too or… If he's not dead, then maybe I'm not dead. While he considered the possibilities, a beam of dim light pierced through as Father Mike, sitting on a wooden chair, moved the blanket enough to expose Paddy's forehead and eyes. Paddy adjusted his eyes, momentarily blinded by the single light bulb hanging from the ceiling. Aunt Joe's hand holding a shot glass of whiskey passed in front of Father Mike. Paddy looked at Aunt Joe.

"Here, boy, drink this. It'll warm you up."

Paddy drank the whiskey and felt the burn going down. Aunt Joe rolled him on his back, fluffed the pillows, and slightly propped him up. Paddy looked around. Everyone was gone except for Aunt Joe, Peg, Father Mike, and the bishop. The fireplace was burning bright, and a strong wind could be heard howling outside. Paddy glanced at Father Mike.

"Paddy, my child...we heard you'd fallen ill, and myself and Bishop Flynn here wanted to visit you and say a few special prayers for you...if that's alright with you, Paddy."

"Yes, Father, yes, anything..." A cough interrupted Paddy followed by a shiver and more wheezing.

"Yes, Father, prayers."

"Special prayers it is, then, for young Paddy."

Father Mike stood up from the chair. Paddy looked at the bishop, a man much older than Father Mike with grey hair. Both holy men were dressed in traditional black. Paddy watched Father Mike move the chair to the kitchen table by the back wall. The bishop followed. Paddy intently watched them opening a bag and taking an assortment of things out. He watched them both put on violet-colored scarves, otherwise known as vestments or stoles, around their necks. Although Paddy had been an altar boy, he had never seen the violet-colored scarf.

Father Mike and Bishop Flynn turned away from the table and walked toward Paddy, side by side as if in a parade or military march. The sight gave Paddy an odd feeling, causing goosebumps, that he didn't understand. They stood by his bed, the bishop holding a Bible and Father Mike holding a small round tin. Paddy looked up at them in their violet stoles, curious.

"Father Mike, I've never seen that color before. Why is it different?"

A slight smile hid their somber expression as Father Mike hesitated answering.

"Well, Paddy, I'll tell you...this color is called violet, and it's a special color for special prayers...special prayers like the ones we're going to pray for you...and that's why Bishop Flynn is here to say extra special prayers for you."

The bishop smiled in agreement as he regarded Paddy.

"Yes Paddy, special prayers for you."

Paddy was overwhelmed, beaming, and noticed a tear in Father Mike's eye—a tear of joy, Paddy assumed.

"Alright, Paddy, we're going to begin now...alright?"

"Alright, Father."

"In the name of the Father..."

Paddy watched and listened as the clerical duo incanted an assortment of prayers, their Irish accents blending in the Latin recitations. During the ceremonial prayers, Father Mike dabbed his thumb in the tin, which contained an oil, and rubbed his thumb on Paddy's forehead while reciting in Latin. Paddy thought it must be a special oil for the special prayers. During the prayers, Paddy paid attention and often found himself praying,  pretending in his mind to be a priest and praying in Latin, all the while fighting the continuous bouts of shivering, wheezing, and sweats.

When the prayers ended, Father Mike and the bishop packed away their vestments and the tin of oil. Paddy listened to them talk with Aunt Joe and Peg, although his state of mind did not cooperate in understanding what they were saying, but he had a strong inclination that they were talking about him. Aunt Joe offered Father Mike and the bishop hot cups of tea before they left. Father Mike noticed Paddy watching them and he walked over to Paddy.

"Would you like a sip of tea, Paddy?"

He nodded in assent, and Father Mike gave Paddy a sip, to which he reacted with a surprised smile.

"You like it?"

"Good...it's real good."

Paddy took a few more sips, unusual for him being he never liked tea before. It tasted good and gave him a warming feeling similar to the whiskey, although Paddy thought the whiskey tasted much better. A few minutes later, Father Mike and the bishop said their goodbyes to Paddy and left.

Aunt Joe and Peg finished up their tea, and Peg went to the back room to go to bed while Aunt Joe tidied up. After she finished tidying up and restocking the fire, she made a last check on Paddy and headed to turn off the light. As she approached the light switch, there was a knock on the door.

THE LAST VISITOR

Paddy watched Aunt Joe answer the door and heard a faint exchange of words. Another visitor entered.

"Thank you for letting me visit... I'm sorry for the late hour, but I heard about young Paddy and wanted to stop by and check on him."

The voice sounded familiar, a woman's voice. She chatted with Aunt Joe for a moment as she pulled the hood of her greyish-green cloak off her head, revealing red hair. The sight of the red-haired glowing woman ignited memories of the encounters with the Banshee and made Paddy anxious. His anxiety grew as the woman locked eyes with Paddy and approached.

"I promise I'll only be a few minutes and say a prayer with Paddy, and then I'll be on my way."

Paddy nervously watched the smiling woman. He was struck speechless, too nervous to say anything or know what to say as she walked over to him. He was still unsure who or what she was, never had an explanation about that night he first saw her, or knew what she wanted or if her intent was to harm or help him. Before he knew it, the woman was sitting next to him. As she sat down, the ceiling light went out, giving Paddy a fright. The room was slightly illuminated from the fire and the woman's dimly radiating hair. At the woman's request, Aunt Joe had turned out the light.

"Thank you, Josephine... You go off to bed now, and I'll let myself out."

Paddy incredulously watched Aunt Joe leave the room and then he turned back to the woman smiling down on him as she tenderly placed a hand on his head.

"Now, now, Paddy, not to worry, it's all right... Just close your eyes and let me say a little prayer for you."

Paddy was shaking with nerves and a fever. The woman's caress of his head was comforting, and he did as he was told and closed his eyes. He felt the woman move closer to him, bend down next to his ear, and begin to whisper. He did not understand nor barely hear it. The whisper wasn't the blended English language with the Irish accent ramblings he so often had difficulty understanding; this was different. The unintelligible whispered prayer continued for a minute or more.

Paddy experienced a new sense of panic when he realized that the woman had both of her hands his head. The whispering continued, and Paddy's imagination ran wild. *Was this some sort of mad satanic incantation, or was it something else?* Then he noticed that the blackness under his eyelids grew bright. His eyes were still closed tight, but there was light. Paddy began to work on his courage, his fearlessness, to open his eyes, or at least peek. As he sneakily squinted, he was momentarily blinded. Nothing but white light. He tried again but more slowly to allow his eyes to focus. He pretended to keep his eyes closed while squinting so that the woman would not catch him. He peeked again, noticing the light was coming from the woman, just like it did before, but this time her eyes were closed, her hair was standing up, floating in a brightness that illuminated the whole room.

"I told you to close your eyes."

"Sorry."

The glowing stopped and the woman's hair, in seemingly slow motion, fell down. She abruptly stood up and walked to the door.

"It will be alright, Paddy... See you soon."

She opened the door, letting a gust of wind blow through the house, and with the wind, two ravens flew in. They found their way to a rafter as the woman closed the door behind her.

What did she mean, see you soon?

Paddy pulled the covers up over his head and burrowed down. His imagination, combined with the anxiety, went to work on what it all meant. *Maybe it was some satanic incarnation and she's coming back to get me. That night when she argued with the banshee, maybe they were fighting over which one of them was gonna get me. And what the bloody hell is with the ravens? It makes sense now, yep, it all makes sense. They work for the glowing woman and made sure the Banshee did not get me first. But she's a banshee too, right? They both want to take me...just waiting for me to die. That's why they came here.*

Paddy's imagination continued to ramble, thinking of different scenarios until the earlier shot of whiskey started to take its effect on him, and he slowly drifted off to sleep with revolving images of the woman, the special prayers, the violet stoles, imagining himself as a priest, and those ravens perched in the rafter that he figured were staring down at him. His thoughts and dreams drifted with the howling wind and clattering of bushes and rain hitting the windows. Later, he briefly woke up when Aunt Joe, wrapped in a blanket, sat down by his feet. The ceiling light was off, and the room was dimly illuminated by the fireplace. He fell back to sleep as quickly as he awoke, back to his dreams.

Sometime later, a strong gust of wind hit the house and woke Paddy up. The wind seemed to reverberate throughout the house. He peaked out from under the blanket. The fire was still going, and Aunt Joe was asleep by his feet, which Paddy found odd. *She never sleeps there.*

ANOTHER LAST VISITOR

A bang on the door startled Paddy and Aunt Joe out of their sleep. Joe sat up, slightly disoriented for a moment and irritated.

"What was that?"

Paddy didn't answer and looked at the window that mimicked a television screen playing the varying shades of a stormy sky and the flickering of distant lightning.

Another bang on the door caused another startle.

"Christ!" Aunt Joe yelled out, angrily standing up and mumbling to herself as she shuffled to the door. Paddy remained hunkered down under the blankets but watchful.

She opened the door, allowing a gust of wind to enter the house, accompanied by the cold and noise of the stormy weather. The brisk air hit Paddy's face and the noise muffled Aunt Joe's reaction.

"Jesus, Mary, and Joseph!"

Paddy listened, stunned. The brief blasphemy from Aunt Joe did not sound as if she was afraid or fearful. To Paddy's ears, it sounded like she was surprised, as if she recognized who, or what, was at the door. The blankets around Paddy's head blocked out any distinguishable words between Aunt Joe and the visitor in the doorway. Paddy pulled back the blanket in an effort to hear. The door remained open, so he could not hear anything except the wind blowing through the house. Paddy felt the cold of the night air and wondered why Aunt Joe stood, apparently frozen, for so long in the open doorway.

Finally, Aunt Joe stepped back from the door and allowed the visitor to enter. The visitor was unrecognizable, a dark, cloaked figure in the shadow cast by the fire.

The figure and Aunt Joe walked to the fire, and he faintly heard a soft-spoken woman's voice.

"You're a saint, letting me in out of this weather."

Paddy was curious about who it was, peaking through the blanket. Aunt Joe did not answer the visitor but did acknowledge her with an approving nod. They stood for a few moments facing the fire, warming up.

"I heard about young Paddy's fright with his ills and wanted to pay a visit."

Aunt Joe nodded but did not answer.

"Would it be alright if I sat by Paddy for a spell and kept him company?"

Aunt Joe momentarily hesitated.

"I'll get the light."

Aunt Joe quickly crossed the room toward the light switch on the wall by Paddy and the couch.

"Let it be! Let the boy sleep! I just want to sit by him and say a prayer."

Aunt Joe stopped with fear overtaking her face in reaction to the visitor's tone, which sounded more like a command than a request.

Aunt Joe headed to the kitchen table to grab a chair for the visitor. Paddy noticed a look of worry on her face. The voice stirred a faint memory, similar to one he knew but not entirely recognizable. *Was it the Banshee, or the glowing woman again, or...?* He didn't know; nerves overtook him. Paddy never understood if the glowing woman was a Banshee in disguise arguing with the other Banshee over his soul. The presence of the ravens inside the house, perched on a rafter overlooking the room, added to the developing unease.

Paddy's imagination went to work, his shivers and fever a forgotten agony overtaken by sudden concern and wondering if the Banshee was back. Paddy jumped from a simultaneous caw of the ravens with a flash of lightning, revealing the sight of a reaper, sickle in hand, outside the window.

Speechless, Paddy grimaced, tightened up under his blankets, and scooted firmly against the back of the couch. Concern and wondering withdrew, overtaken by terror. He glanced at the woman facing the fireplace and then to Aunt Joe bringing the chair to his bedside. He let his fears and imagination overtake him, panicking as his eyes darted from Aunt Joe to the figure, the ravens in the ceiling, the window, and back again.

Aunt Joe put the chair by the couch, turned and walked halfway to the fireplace, and stopped, as if she was waiting for another command from the visitor.

"You can go off to bed now, Josephine... I'll stay with the boy and let myself out."

Paddy watched Aunt Joe stand still for a short time.

"Go on now, Josephine."

Aunt Joe paused and then, as if under a charm or spell, walked to the back-room entry in the far corner and entered the back bedroom.

What the hell?! Paddy shouted to himself, *Don't leave me here.* Paddy was alone with the visitor, a visitor who remained facing the fireplace and had yet to show her face, which Paddy, believing the visitor could be the Banshee, did not want to see. Paddy's imagination, as usual, was in full speed, recounting the previous encounters, evaluating options, possibilities, and even escape routes. The back room was not an escape option because it had no doors or windows, although he briefly considered hiding under a bed to be a plausible alternative until he remembered those long arms of the Banshee that stretched out like tree limbs. The back window over the kitchen table was too narrow, but the front window...the front window was big enough, but, he calculated, climbing out the window might provide the Banshee with an opportunity to grab him. Giving the Banshee any opportunity was not an option. The only escape was the door. His mind's ramblings escalated with wondering if she was a Banshee or some other sort of creature, like a witch or a Reaper, in disguise. The possibilities were endless in Paddy's mind as he kept a close eye on the visitor, who created a sense of uneasiness as she continued to face the fire in silence. The storm outside raged on, the strong gusts of wind howled, and brief flashes of lightning filled the front window, all reminiscent of a scary scene Paddy remembered from years earlier in an Abbot and Costello movie.

"I know you're awake over there, Paddy!"

A strong gust of house-shaking wind and a lightning flash coincided perfectly with the comment and threw Paddy into panicky overdrive. He pushed himself into the corner of the couch, holding tightly onto the blankets, while resisting, unsuccessfully, an increase of wheezing. He recognized this feeling, and it was intensifying. *I can't breathe, I can't breathe.*

Then he said it out loud, as best as he could, although not loud enough for Aunt Joe or Peg to hear, "I can't breathe. I can't breathe."

A sinister, chastising voice asked, "Did you say something, Paddy?"

Anxiety, panic, and wheezing took control of Paddy and kept him frozen in the corner of the couch, waiting for what was next. The visitor finally turned, although her face was still obscured by the darkness and shadows cast by the fire. Paddy's wheezing combined with sudden trembling, and even though Paddy could not see her, he knew the visitor was looking at him, staring at him; he could feel it.

"I see you over there, Paddy... I see you curled up in that corner."

He remained frozen. His mind ran out of options, except for, *Dear God, please help, please help me.*

Another gust of wind and some bushes hitting the front window broke his concentration. Sometimes a fire can cast false shadows, making things that stand still appear to move and things that are moving appear to move faster, or slower. Paddy was focused on the visitor who didn't move, but for a moment, it looked like she did, until another gust of wind caused Paddy to look out the window and within that brief glance, Paddy's fear grew at the sight of the Reaper. He looked back at the visitor. *She had moved! Much closer.*

Light from the fire on the wall behind Paddy reflected onto the face of the visitor. It *was* the Banshee, smiling in silence with a grey-faced, grotesque expression, increasing the silent tension. Paddy tried to fight, but his weakened condition was an accomplice to the Banshee, allowing her to rip the blankets off of him and grab him tightly by his shoulders.

Paddy's wheezing increased far more than he'd ever experienced. The Banshee had a firm grasp of his shoulders, and despite his attempts, Paddy was unable to beat her away. It was hopeless. He was weak, tired, and scared, and felt as if he was screaming, but he was not. All he was doing was wheezing.

"I've got you now, boy."

"Please God!"

"God's not going to help you, Paddy."

"No, no, no! Stop it. Stop it!"

"Let's go, Paddy. It's time to go."

The Banshee was gleeful in her conquest, as Paddy felt himself being elevated and made a futile attempt to grab the back of the couch. The Banshee held him over her head, which placed Paddy with a vantage point to observe the two ravens on the rafter quietly standing, positioning themselves side by side, and spreading their wings. The illumination from the fireplace cast a giant shadow of the dual set of wings on the wall behind Paddy. He turned toward the wall, a move that caught the Banshee's attention.

"What da blazes?"

The Banshee snarled and turned her head toward the ravens as she saw them dropped from the rafter, wings spread wide, silently glide at her. It only took a second as Paddy heard the first flap of the ravens' wings accompanied by a triple caw, caw, caw as one of the ravens landed on the banshee's right shoulder and impaled it with its long talons. The other raven furiously flapped its wings around the Banshee's head, pecking at her with its beak. Paddy fell to the couch and kept his eyes on the Banshee yelling and fighting with the ravens.

Although it had become customary for Paddy to analyze and momentarily delay any action in a situation like this, that was not his reaction this time. He had learned from his previous experiences that there was no time to delay and immediately leapt off the couch, avoiding the banshee's lunge at him trying to prevent his escape. He pushed past the banshee without hesitation or looking back and ran to the door. He pulled on the door handle just as the door was blown open by a deafening gust of wind.

Paddy stumbled out of the door, falling to his knees, squinting against the wind and rain hitting his face. He looked up. The reaper, holding its sickle, stood only feet away in front of him, faceless under the hooded cloak, just like his grandpa had described him. The fight inside the house continued with the Banshee screaming and screeching along with the ravens' caws. Paddy was overcome with a sudden, unexplainable calmness. He wasn't wheezing anymore, and so he thought, *This is it, I'm dead.*

He looked at the Reaper, fearless, for what felt like a long time, although in reality it was just a few seconds, until the sky lit up from lightning. Another cloaked figure approached from behind the Reaper, and Paddy's calmness departed. The reaper briefly glanced over its shoulder and stepped aside, allowing the figure to approach Paddy. He looked up at the figure, the hood empty, just like the Reaper, until a dim glow of orangish-white light shone from inside the hood, accompanied by a voice.

"You're all right, Paddy. Everything's all right... No need to run this time."

Each word spoken increased the brightness, gradually exposing the angelic, radiant smile of the red-haired woman. The glowing woman turned her attention to inside the door. She pulled back her hood, exposing her glowing red hair, intensifying the brightness around her head.

The ongoing battle inside the house and the screeching of the Banshee suddenly stopped. The ravens flew out the front door, sounding off a few caws. The glowing woman moved into the house, and although Paddy had not previously noticed this, he saw that the woman did not walk—she glided or floated.

Paddy's recollections of the woman previously floating was abruptly interrupted by the screaming of the Banshee.

"He's mine, he's mine, he's mine!"

"He's not yours. It's not his time now, and you know that, Banshee!"

The Banshee screeched in anger, infuriating the glowing woman. Paddy and the Reaper heard the glowing woman respond with a deafening screech of her own that blended with a sound resembling echoing trumpets. The inside of the house lit up with a brightness that was so intense it forced Paddy and the Reaper to turn away from the light. Paddy and the Reaper were side by side, their backs turned away from the house. Paddy looked up at the Reaper and it looked at Paddy, slightly shaking its head in what Paddy interpreted as disappointment. The Reaper walked—or glided, as Paddy now noticed—to the other side of the road as the light from the house dimmed and then vanished. The Reaper turned toward Paddy and gestured with his slightly raised sickle, as if it to say, "until next time." The Reaper dissolved into the night mist.

A sense of calm returned to Paddy while he remained on his knees in the wind and misty rain in front of the open door. He was cold, but it felt different; it was a true cold, a normal cold felt from the wind and rain, not the pneumonia-driven chills and shivers from the fever he'd endured for a week. He took a deep breath, the wheezing gone. *Thank you, God, thank you.*

"Jesus, Mary, and Joseph, Paddy, what are you doing?! Get in here! You'll catch your death."

He stood up and gave Aunt Joe a hug in the doorway, then Paddy broke the hug and ran to the shed by the side of the house. Aunt Joe yelled at him to get inside and watched with amazement as he returned from the shed with his arms filled with firewood. She followed him back inside and watched him stock the fire. Paddy felt refreshed, the wheezing completely gone. He dried out by the fire, going over in his mind what had happened and thanking God over and over.

Aunt Joe sat by the fire across from Paddy, speechless, not believing her eyes. She was told by the doctor and Father Mike to expect Paddy's passing that night. The only rational explanation Aunt Joe could think of for Paddy's recovery was that it was a miracle. The overwhelming feeling of joy and thanking God for the miracle overshadowed Aunt Joe's vague dreamlike recollection of the last visitor and wondering how she had ended up in her bed after falling asleep on the couch next to Paddy.

REPRESSION IN PROGRESS

The next morning, Paddy woke up refreshed, no longer feeling sick or having trouble with his asthma. The previous night seemed surreal, and everything was as if nothing out of the ordinary had happened. Remember, Paddy was fearless, and the traumatic and repressed experience with the Banshee in Ireland did not erase his propensity to be mischievous, curious, and attracted to what others may find harmful or dangerous. Some might suspect he had a shine, otherwise known as a gift or divine protection.

As the weeks passed and fall changed to winter, the unspoken questions of Aunt Joe, Aunt Peg, Father Mike, and others about how a ten-year-old boy who they believed would die that night had fully recovered went unanswered. Paddy continued school, his altar boy duties, and his adventures. He helped with his sister and would later remember a trip to nearby Kilkenny where a picture of him and his sister was taken. Everything seemed all right, at least outwardly, but internally, something quietly bothered Paddy.

Paddy knew that the Banshee only appeared near death. He knew the Banshee had appeared three times, first when McCullough died and the second time when his grandpa died. The third time was for Paddy, but he had escaped. The banshee tried again, and failed again, but Paddy had a lingering feeling that the Banshee would try again. The salute of the Reaper's sickle reinforced that theory and added to the urgency to leave Ireland.

Before full repression took hold, Paddy wondered why the ravens kept watch over him. Perhaps they noticed his act of kindness to a brother raven on the field of crows, or they were in the service of something more reverent, divine, or angelic. Paddy now truly believed the glowing woman to be his Guardian Angel who delivered him from evil and kept watch over him throughout his life. Paddy would wonder how else to explain how he had survived that night, that week of pneumonia.

Repression has many layers camouflaged by other layers taking form through imagination, television, exploring castles, attending school, letters from his mother, time with friends, or a growing attachment to an uncle named Jimmy who made the occasional visit with his wife from London. In the spring of 1967, shortly after Paddy's eleventh birthday, Jimmy and his wife paid a visit, which went well until it was time to leave. When Jimmy said goodbye and started to get into the car, Paddy cried and begged Jimmy to take him with them. This was a memory that remained with Paddy: the sight of Jimmy, a grown man, crying, clearly heartbroken with not being able to take Paddy with him. During Paddy's crying tantrum, he watched a passionate discussion between Jimmy and Aunt Joe, a discussion that Paddy would recall entailed Jimmy trying to convince Aunt Joe to allow him to take Paddy...or at least, that was how Paddy liked to think the conversation went.

RUNAWAY

Within weeks of Jimmy's departure, the fantasy-driven imagination of Paddy's mind brewed, and he baked an idea of leaving the middle of rural Ireland to run away to London to live with Jimmy. Tugging of heartstrings or even a chuckle may occur when hearing of a plan like this one— a wild and youthful imagination at work. Normally this kind of story would be just that—imagination and a story. Did Paddy know where Jimmy lived or his address? No, he did not. He did know Jimmy's first and last name and figured he would just ask someone for an address. How would he get there? His plan was to walk and hitchhike the 69.65 miles (again, the marvels of Google later provided this accurate distance) from home to the port of Dublin. Did he know for sure there was a port in Dublin? No, he did not. He assumed there was based on his memory of arriving in Ireland, but he did not know that the Galway port was on the opposite side of the country from Dublin. But that was the plan: to get to Dublin and get on a ship heading to London.

Did Paddy ever make it to London? No, he did not, but he did make it to Dublin. Yes, on a late afternoon, Paddy started walking. He did not pack a bag, did not say goodbye, and his only provision was a bread and butter sandwich for the journey. He walked, and walked, and walked. During this time in Ireland, cars were not common, therefore during his walk, he did not see a car to ask for a ride. Paddy was fearless and determined on his trek, even though it was getting dark. Then he heard a truck coming up behind him and turned around. The sun was setting in the horizon as the truck approached and actually stopped to give a just-turned-eleven-year-old boy a ride. This was a particular moment that Paddy would reflect on later in life that to his belief that he had a Guardian Angel.

The truck ride lasted an hour or so, during which time Paddy shared with the man driving the truck his plans to go to London on a ship. The sun had long set when the truck pulled up to a dock area next to a ship. Paddy jumped out of the truck, thanked the driver, who wished him good luck, and then watched the truck drive off. Paddy paced the lot next to the giant cargo ship, contemplating how he would get on the ship. Did he know the ship was going to London? No, he did not, but that was not going to stop him. His mission was to get on the ship.

A ladder alongside the ship was the only access, and Paddy figured he could climb that very tall ladder. He was fearless. The next obstacle was not being seen. He watched and waited for an opportunity, and as he was making his move, he was interrupted by two approaching policemen.

Had those policemen been two minutes later, Paddy would have made it on to that ship. His failure to get on the ship was more proof that Paddy had a Guardian Angel, although the logical deduction was that the truck driver likely contacted the police.

Paddy was taken to the police station, where he sat on a bench in the lobby. The policemen were nice and gave him snacks, and he eventually fell asleep on the bench until a conversation at the police desk woke him up. It was his Aunt Joe and a man talking to the police sergeant.

Paddy sat up and looked at Aunt Joe, who looked back at him with disappointment on her face. When the conversation with the police sergeant ended, Aunt Joe motioned for Paddy to come along. Oddly, nothing was said or asked by Aunt Joe other than what was he doing. He answered, "Going to Uncle Jimmy's," a reply that Paddy thought generated a slight smile from Aunt Joe. Maybe she understood. Paddy got in the car and his mind slipped into reviewing and examining his failed escape mission.

It had not occurred to Paddy at the time how quickly Aunt Joe came to get him and given the only telephone or car for miles was at Butler's Pub, an assumption can be made that an immediate effort of some kind had taken place to find the missing Paddy and that the police were notified.

Paddy's attempted escape from Ireland to his Uncle Jimmy's had been foiled, and his life went back to normal, back to school for a few more weeks while looking forward to the approaching summer adventures.

Something still lingered in his mind, just as it did after the night he was supposed to die. Paddy's practice of repression was always working to suppress the flashes of his bouts with the Banshee and the waiting Reaper. Paddy experienced increasing anxiety and fear of the approaching fall boxing practice and the walks home at night. He thought about quitting boxing, but the repressing voices in his head questioned his logic. Still, something lingered.

PART II

NEW YORK CITY: LEAVING THE MYTHICAL BEHIND

After his escape attempt to Dublin, Paddy's mother arrived a month later for a short visit and shortly thereafter returned to the United States with Paddy, without his sister. It was summer of 1967 for the eleven-year-old to begin a new adventure living with his mother in apartment 4F on East 77th Street in the Yorkville area of Manhattan.

The arrival in New York City was surreal for Paddy, but it didn't take long for him to adapt to his new surroundings and the streets of New York. The sounds of the city were a constant, and the new neighborhood was full of adventures and news friends.

Paddy would see his dad occasionally, and the first time seeing each other, his dad cried, but it was not because of the emotional reconnection, although that was there, but because Paddy's appearance shocked him—a far too skinny, frail kid. Paddy's introduction to hamburgers, French fries, pizza, and Chinese dim sum would soon get a hold of him. His mother's new husband did not live with them and Paddy saw him on occasion, but a divorce was in progress. Otherwise, Paddy had no negative memories of the relationship.

A Life Lesson

The summer of 1967 on the Upper East Side of Yorkville, Manhattan, was a new environment and learning experience for Paddy. His mother introduced him to the neighborhood, including the nearby Carl Schurz Park on East End Avenue, where Paddy would frequent over the summer. Paddy adjusted quickly to his new environment. He discovered a corner deli on York Avenue and Seventy-Seventh Street, where he was introduced to a product that many believe, even today, does not have an expiration date. That product was Hostess Twinkies, a treasure for the price of ten cents, and a bottle of Coke for another ten cents.

Clearly, Paddy's mother wanted him to be happy and have a higher standard of living than he experienced in Ireland. His mother introduced him to color television, the radio, a record player, and a gold-colored bicycle, which Paddy instantly fell in love with. Paddy rode his bike throughout the Yorkville area and nearby Schultz Park. Paddy loved his bicycle.

A week after receiving the bicycle, Paddy rode the bicycle in Carl Schurz Park and made a stop at the path that bordered the overlook of the East River. He had vivid memories of the river, which was dirty and littered with trash. While gazing at the river, Paddy was approached by two boys who were a few years older than he was. They were friendly and started a conversation. One of the boys admired the bicycle and asked Paddy if he could take it for a ride. Of course, the naïve and friendly Paddy, not wanting to be rude, agreed, and the boy took the bicycle for a ride while his friend remained with Paddy. A few minutes passed without the boy with the bike returning, and Paddy grew concerned. The boy's friend also acted concerned and told Paddy that he was going to look for his friend, but that Paddy should stay there in case the other boy returned. The boys did not return. The reality sank in that the boys had stolen his bicycle, and it devastated Paddy. He sulked, cried, and was heartbroken.

Paddy walked home, crying all the way. He entered the apartment crying, and his mother asked what was wrong. Paddy told his mother what happened. He didn't recall if his mother said anything; however, he did remember she was very upset. His mother left the apartment without a word, except to tell him to stay there.

Paddy stayed in the apartment, upset, and continued crying. He sat by the window on the fire escape overlooking the street. Half an hour later, Paddy glanced down at the street and saw his mother approaching the building with a bicycle. Paddy didn't know what to think. Maybe she had found the bike. Two minutes later, she entered the apartment with a new, gold colored bicycle. Paddy was ecstatic, and his mother had a smile on her face.

The average parent might have reacted differently in this situation, telling their child, "Tough Luck," and definitely would not have bought a replacement bicycle within half an hour. Paddy's mother's reaction was different, likely an emotional response to her naïve son being taken advantage of.

Paddy was admittedly very naïve and had a lot to learn about life and living in New York City. Paddy learned his first valuable lesson that day and was introduced to the importance of reading people and street smarts, a skill he quickly acquired.

St. Stephens Elementary Days

In September 1967, Paddy's mother enrolled him in St. Stephen's of Hungary Catholic elementary school on East 82nd Street. Paddy's age would normally have him starting sixth grade; however, the Irish primary school had not sufficiently prepared him, and he was placed in the fourth grade, two years behind his peers of the same age. Paddy made the daily five-block walk to school and was introduced to  the Principal, Sister Mercedes, Sister Jude, and a roster of other nuns all of whom taught various subjects.

The first official introduction began with an introduction to Mrs. Francis, the teacher of the fourth-grade class. Another introduction was to the traditional hunt and purchase of the classic Catholic school uniform, which for St. Stephen's was a green jacket, grey pants, and a white dress shirt that required a clip-on red checkered tie. Paddy's assimilation into school was easy, and while being a few years older may have been an advantage, it seemed unnoticed by his classmates, and he made friends quickly. Within a day he was given the temporary nickname of "Irish" due his Irish accent, which he lost after a couple years.

One of the main activities during recess and lunchtime was the all-time city classic street sport of stickball, a creative endeavor utilizing a broom handle, hence the "stick," and a Spalding brand high-bounce pinkish-colored rubber ball. Stickball was similar in many ways to baseball rules; manhole covers, trashcan lids, bumpers of a parked car, or the curb were used for bases, accompanied by the occasional verbal warning "Car" that bellowed out upon the approach of any oncoming car on the one-way street.

Lunchtime was half an hour, and there were three options: bringing lunch, buying lunch at school, or eating at the Diner at the corner of 82nd Street and York Avenue. Paddy and a few of his friends made the one-minute sprint from the school to the corner. Paddy ordered a hamburger and French fries with a Coke for the low menu price of about a dollar. Paddy and his friends were regulars for most school days and had standing orders that were ready upon their arrival. The diner owner was a very nice man, and his name eluded Paddy, although Jimmy seemed to stand out.

Paddy had never experienced a school environment where there were nuns, a situation that took some getting used to. Paddy had fond memories of his five years at St Stephen's. The nuns were, for the most part, the stereotypical stern disciplinarians; however, the stereotype would be considered unfair by most Catholic school alumni, although there are those who would disagree.

Discipline, yes, and Paddy witnessed a few instances of "hold your hands out, palms up," and the administering of five or ten wacks with a wooden ruler across the hands. Except for the receiver of the wacks, most Catholic kids found it difficult to restrain themselves from quiet, unidentified giggles. When most receivers of the punishment  walked back to their seats, they were often observed projecting an unceremonious smile. It should be noted that the lack of tears in most instances may have been due to the level of intensity, or lack of intensity that the wacks were administered. It was rare that wacks were supercharged, producing a river of tears, and it could be said that it was smacks versus wacks that were given. It was not uncommon to observe an occasional smile of amusement from the nun administering the punishment.

During his second year at St. Stephen's in 1968, the nuns took Paddy's class on a ten-block walk for a field trip to a movie theater to see The Sound of Music. On that day, Paddy and his classmates were exposed to an unseen side of the nuns they had never imagined or knew was possible— the carefully hidden human side. That day revealed that, beneath their traditional black and white habits and stern, disciplined exterior appearances, the nuns could smile, interact with one another and the students, and have fun. Stereotypes aside, the nuns were real people under their habits.

During the first couple of years at St. Stephen's, Paddy joined the Boy Scouts, attended the meetings, and during the summer, attended the summer camps. His interest in the Boy Scouts diminished after a few years due to getting a delivery boy job, moving in with his dad, taking karate classes, and witnessing hazing by the scoutmaster, his assistants, and a few older boys during a summer camp evening at a campfire. Paddy admittedly was a bit naïve to the whole concept of hazing and the practice of hazing the new boys in the troop. Not all of the new boys were hazed, including Paddy, and it seemed to Paddy that the younger more vulnerable boys were picked on for hazing. The hazing consisted of verbal abuse while forcibly stripping a boy naked and covering him in shaving cream. Most boys ended up in tears and were humiliated, which, apparently, based on the enjoyment and laughter of the administrators of the hazing, was the sad objective.

St. Stephen's parish participated in the CYO, the Catholic Youth Organization, and had a basketball team that Paddy joined. The basketball team was coached by Father Edmund. Paddy liked playing basketball, although he was not all that great at it, and by the sixth and seventh grades, his two-year advantage over his peers resulted in him being a bit taller and being drafted to play the center position. Paddy would have liked to continue playing on the team, but the move to his dad's, karate, and the delivery boy job limited his time.

Paddy's experience at St. Stephen's were an essential positive part of Paddy's young life that was set aside from other events outside of school.

In June 1972, the just-turned sixteen-year-old Paddy and his classmates graduated eighth grade from St. Stephen of Hungary on East 82nd Street. In preparation for graduation, pictures were taken, and looking back, Paddy will admit to  taking a far too serious graduation picture.

But the Radio Rolled Me

The exposure to the Monkees on the small black and white television in Ireland had been a spark for a love of music for Paddy, although there are those who would disagree that the what the Monkees did was music. Within weeks of his arrival in New York in the summer of 1967 his mother gave him the popular handheld AM/FM transistor radio that

had an unlimited selection of music all day. That little radio that was powered by the that little nine-volt battery seemed to play forever and was one of Paddy's treasures.

The first song Paddy remembered hearing —which, coincidentally, he found to be symbolic of his arrival to New York—was "Downtown" by Petula Clark. There were many more songs that he loved and a few months later in November his

mother bought him a record player and the start of collecting the seven inch diameter small 45 RPM records began. The 45 records had just on song on each side and the first one Paddy remembered receiving from his mother was the Beatles, "I Am

the Walrus", "Hello Goodbye." Paddy had a distinct memory of his mother's excitement introducing him to the record player and playing "I am the Walrus." There would be a lot more records over the next couple of years.

Paddy was ahead of his time in 1967 reflecting on the lyrics of the 1974 song *Life Is a Rock (But the Radio Rolled Me)*. Aside from school, television and other activities Paddy found the perfect companion with the transistor AM radio to aid him with his introverted tendencies.

Watching television in the evenings was the other obsession for Paddy. He loved the science fiction shows, *Star Trek*, and *Lost in Space*, but he also loved the variety shows, *The Carol Burnett Show*, and he especially liked the *Smothers Brothers* and *Ed Sullivan*, and in 1968 *Laugh In*.

Paddy watched television on a much bigger television than the twelve-inch black and white television he had watched in Ireland. The bigger nineteen-inch color console television was a dramatic change, although many shows were still in black and white.  Seeing a television in color was an amazing sight and NBC announced their color shows with a phrase "In Living Color" accompanying the NBC Peacock.

A year later, April 4, 1968, he watched the news about the Martin Luther King Jr. assassination and the riots that followed. On June 5, 1968, he also watched the Robert F. Kennedy assignation unfold on television.

Paddy adopted a love for sports and quickly became a fan of the New York Jets football team, their star quarterback, Joe Namath, and their 1969 Super Bowl win. His favorite team was baseball's New York Mets, and while he currently resides in St. Louis and roots for the St. Louis Cardinals, Paddy holds a special place in his heart

Miracle Mets

for the New York Mets, who were also called the Miracle Mets in 1969, winning the World Series that year. The New York Knicks basketball team was another favorite that won the 1970 and 1973 championships. It was an exciting time for New York sports fans.

The first few years living with his mother went well for Paddy as he attended school, joined Boy Scouts, made friends, and seen his dad on occasion. He watched television, including the news, and became an avid reader of newspapers and magazines, keeping up with everything including sports stats.

As the months passed during that first year, Paddy adjusted to a sense of normalcy and eventually became what was known as a latchkey kid. His mother was home during the daytime and left for work in the evenings. Sometimes his mother's girlfriends would stop by, and they left together to go to work. Paddy fondly remembers that his mother and her friends were always dressed nicely in their dresses, makeup, and jewelry, reminding him of models. Paddy's mother always made sure he did not go hungry and made him dinner or left him money to order dinner from either a pizza shop or a Chinese place on the corner of 77th Street and York Avenue.

At some point during early 1968, Paddy's mother rented a second apartment on the third floor of their building, Apt. 3B. Paddy was given a key to the new apartment; however, during this period, his mother transitioned to spending most of her time in the new apartment without Paddy. As it is with many of Paddy's reflections in hindsight, it was as if his mother had attempted to establish a barrier to separate Paddy in apartment 4F from her life in apartment 3B. Here again, repression may have been engaged.

DEMONS AT WORK

Paddy stayed busy with school, friends, music, and television. Sunday was usually a stay-home day unless there was a visit with his dad because, believe it or not, nothing was open on Sunday in New York City. The transition of returning from Ireland in the summer of 1967 to the approaching end of 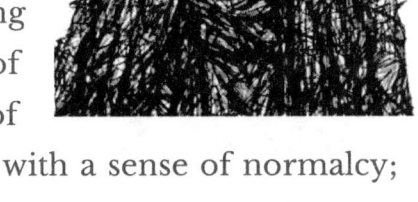 1968 in many ways was routine with a sense of normalcy; however, something was wrong.

Paddy's early training in the art of repression prepared him for future events that would require a continued practice of repression and developing a skill for ignoring the realities that surrounded him while embracing the relationship he had with his mother. Paddy developed a gradual belief that demons had gotten ahold of his mother. He was adept at using his imagination or may have been ignorant or too young to understand his mother's life and the demons that possessed her, which he would not fully understand until years later.

This latchkey kid saw his mother regularly but mostly when he stopped by the third-floor apartment. His dad seemed to visit more often, and there was talk about Paddy moving in with his dad. Paddy mentions hindsight often in his story, and here again with hindsight, he believes his dad had become aware of something that prompted him to arrange for Paddy to move in with him in Astoria, Queens. Another option to consider was that Paddy's mother recognized her demons, and her love for Paddy prompted her to arrange for him to move in with his dad. Paddy preferred to believe that the decision was mutual between his parents.

SENSE OF NORMALCY

The move happened in September of 1968. While Paddy's mother remained in the third-floor apartment in Manhattan, Paddy made the move to his dad's apartment in Astoria, Queens. He maintained the life he had grown accustomed to in Manhattan. He stayed in the same school for four more years. Paddy became a skilled traveler of the subway, buses, and streets of New York City, making the daily commute to school from Ditmars Station in Astoria to East 86th Street and Lexington Avenue to get to school. He

also added ice skating to his activities and made weekend trips to Rockefeller Center ice rink and the Central Park ice rink, where he developed a taste for the famous New York pretzels.

What Clock?

Paddy's dad took him to the occasional movie, including the 1968 films *2001: A Space Odyssey* and *Planet of the Apes*, but this was after a humorous story Paddy recalled about his dad taking him to Madison Square Garden to see the Ringling Brothers and Barnum & Bailey circus. Paddy was bored and kept asking what time it was. The repetitive question eventually irritated his dad, and he told Paddy to look at the giant clock hanging from the ceiling of the Garden, to which Paddy answered, "What clock?"

After a visual test, his dad discovered that Paddy had developed very bad vision. The following week, a pair of wire-rimmed glasses that were trendy at the time fixed the vision problem.

Pop Pop Boom

Nighttime had already fallen on the bitter cold Friday evening of January 10, 1969. Paddy was in his bedroom around 5:30 doing schoolwork when he heard a loud noise outside the apartment building. The sound was a loud pop, pop, pop followed by a boom that violently shook the building. Paddy and his dad rushed to the front window and saw flames on the roof of the building connected to theirs. Everyone in the surrounding apartments and buildings evacuated to the street and playground area across from the apartments.

Paddy's dad noted that it was a close call, that it was a miracle that the WOR AM-710 traffic helicopter that crashed on top of the building missed their apartment.

Paddy agreed it was a close call—a very close call, missing their top third-floor apartment by about twenty yards—but Paddy thought it wasn't a miracle, it was that Guardian Angel, although it was a miracle that the pilot was the only one killed. The fire department would take several hours to put the fire out, and everyone had to stay outside in the cold.

Paddy remembered it was a very cold night, and they walked around to stay warm. After an hour, as they walked in the open playground area across the street, Paddy saw something on the ground. Paddy instinctively knew what it was and showed his dad. His dad told him to leave it alone, and hid dad told a nearby policeman that the helicopter pilot's torso, clad in an aviator's leather jacket, was on the playground.

Helicopter crash aside, Paddy's new normal was in motion and continued through the rest of 1969. Paddy was excited on Sunday evening of July 20, 1969, to watch the moon landing and Neil Armstrong's first steps on the moon, a moment he would always remember and inspired him to want to become an astronaut, which would not happen due to his poor vision.

A New Yorker Knows

Just like any city or community, only the residents know those unique customs or idiosyncrasies that make them who they are. As a twelve-year-old, Paddy developed into a veteran subway traveler. He quickly adjusted to the morning, cramped subway cars where passengers stood shoulder to shoulder, face to chest, and front to back, invading each other's space, shifting in unison with each other with each choreographed shift and sway of the  subway cars. For those lucky, or unlucky enough to have a seat, they were rewarded with the opportunity to sit and be presented with a multitude of human crotches of varying dimensions, heights, and widths, and on occasion, odors, inches from their face.

There was hope of sorts, a rescue option, so to speak, as heads turned, many in an almost impossible 360-degree rotation in search of the one instrument that was universally used by New Yorkers on the subway to provide a temporary and imaginary escape from the sardine-encased, crotch-infested show. That instrument was the ever-popular and always reliable newspaper, the New York Daily News. The newspaper not only provided news, it provided a shield for the seated passengers, it also provided those with tailored observation skills, the opportunity to take full advantage of the panoramic view provided from any position, sitting, standing, short, or tall.

There was another newspaper, The New York Times, an oversized, space intrusive, and print too small to read without leering or leaning into the beholder of the paper. The Daily News was the most popular, easy to handle, easy to  open. It was the early version of in-person social media, where conversation would start about the previous night's Yankees, Mets, or Knicks game.

Another distraction was the rows of advertisements, floor covered trash, and ever creative graffiti that covered the subway cars, inside and out.

A few days after moving in with his dad, Paddy was introduced to another common New York experience, the New York nuclear war-resistant Cockroach. Paddy seen roaches at his mother's place and they were a familiar scene, however, seeing roaches was a different experience than feeling roaches crawling across his feet under the covers at three in the morning. These roaches were brazen, immune to pesticides, and found in the bottom of shoes and newspapers; they were indestructible and regenerated. Creepy crawlers running across his feet was something

Paddy learned to live with, although tucking the bedclothes in did help.

Taekwondo Karate

Prior to graduating from St. Stephens in 1972 while looking out the window of the elevated RR train over Astoria Boulevard heading home from school, Paddy noticed a sign for a new karate school. Paddy was one of the first students to join the Moon Sung Lee Taekwondo Institute and had the honor of being in Master Lee's first official session on a Saturday morning. Paddy remained a student for two years until the end of 1974. Master Lee and his school has remained a fixture in Astoria and today his son operates the school  under the name Strong Martial Arts.

DELIVERY BOY YEARS

In the spring of 1970, Paddy turned fourteen and a new opportunity presented itself. The legal age in New York to work at that time was fourteen, and Paddy got a part-time job as a delivery boy with the local supermarket chain D'Agostino's on 76th Street and Lexington Avenue. Some of Paddy's fondest memories were the four and a half years he worked at D'Agostino's—or Dag, as it was called by the locals—until the end of 1974.

Paddy had many interesting encounters, experiences, and education working at D'Agostino's over the years. One entertaining memory was on a summer Saturday morning, he watched a balding middle-aged man enter the store singing loudly, put his three-year-old son in a hand basket, and begin strolling through the store swinging the basket, generating tummy-busting giggles from his son and entertaining everyone in the store.

The man, who Paddy recognized, wanted his groceries delivered, and Paddy got the job. Unlike other customers wanting delivery, instead of heading home, the man waited, placed his son on his shoulders, and walked with Paddy conversing with him. Many of the buildings in that neighborhood had a doorman at the front entrance and a separate service entrance for deliveries. Paddy attempted to go to the service entrance, to which the man stopped him and insisted that he accompany him to the front entrance.

The doorman, doing his job, attempted to tell Paddy he had to use the service entrance, but the man sternly insisted that Paddy be allowed to accompany him. After the delivery, Paddy returned to the store and made many future deliveries to the man, who was a well-known actor and comedian named Dom DeLuise, a very nice and funny man who tipped well.

On another occasion, the store manager asked Paddy to assist an elderly customer shop for his groceries. As the shopping and conversation proceeded, Paddy recognized the customer as being Moe Howard of the Three Stooges. Mr. Howard was also a nice man who tipped well.

Another D'Agostino's delivery on a Friday evening was for a man who, upon checking out at the cash register, asked to meet the delivery boy. Paddy was elected, and the man handed Paddy a big tip, said thank you, and then bade goodbye to everyone. It seemed like everyone knew him. It was not until Paddy read the delivery ticket that he saw the

name Tony Curtis. Fifteen minutes later, Paddy arrived at the brownstone house where a teenage girl answered the door. Deliveries to Tony Curtis's house seemed to be a regular weekly event for about a year or so, and Paddy developed an infatuation for the teenage girl who usually answered the door.

Given that Paddy was in the fourteen to sixteen age bracket, no doubt puberty had stricken, helping along with his attraction for the girl. During each delivery, they exchanged brief pleasantries, which were often cut short by an adult woman inside. Paddy's courage on multiple occasions to ask the girl for a date failed to materialize. Paddy knew who the famous actor Tony Curtis was, but at that time, all he knew was he liked the girl who answered the door. However, he never found out if she was the future Hollywood actress Jamie Lee Curtis or her sister Kelly.

DEMONS

As 1970 passed, Paddy paid occasional visits to his mother and he knew something was off. Those demons had a hold. There were occasions when Paddy would greet male visitors, even a detective. It became more evident during visits that something was amiss with his mother. Paddy noticed her tendency to keep the apartment dark, dimly lit, and his mother's head was shaved. As visits progressed, more oddities occurred. She walked around the apartment in long see-through blouses, all modesty eluding her.

His mother used a record player to play records backwards for Paddy and would ask him if he could hear what was being said, if he could hear the messages. Paddy appeased his mother by pretending he could hear them. Room lights were manipulated to cast shadows on the ceiling and walls, and in hindsight, Paddy often recalled pieces of foil and an assortment of other objects on the coffee table.

Paddy's suspicions grew, and given his gained knowledge from television news, magazines, and newspapers about the growing experimentation with LSD psychedelic experiences in the 1960s and 70s, it became evident to Paddy that demons had control of his mother.

After one of the visits, Paddy reluctantly told his dad that he had visited his mother, an answer that upset his dad. Even though his dad was upset, Paddy did tell him that the visit was weird. Paddy's dad told him not to visit his mother anymore, and although he agreed, he continued to visit, but not as frequently.

Paddy's memory on the timing was off, but to him, it seemed that within a month, his dad told him that his mother was in Bellevue Hospital, and he should go visit her.

Notorious Bellevue

The Notorious Bellevue Hospital was well known as a psychiatric hospital, and the word "Bellevue" was

commonly thrown around in jest implying someone belonged in Bellevue. Repression was immediately activated, and Paddy waited until the next Sunday to go to Bellevue on First Avenue in Manhattan.

The subway from Astoria to lower Manhattan took longer on a Sunday, but Paddy was not in a hurry, and if anything, he was reluctant. Repression was working on him, as he didn't want to store any memories of this visit. He exited the subway station and made the ten-block walk to First Avenue and 28th Street. Standing across the street from Bellevue, Paddy was struck by the enormity of the building.

Paddy worked up his courage, crossed the street, and entered the lobby. He asked for directions and navigated the maze within Bellevue, up an elevator, then through more mazes until a metal door.

When Paddy rang the buzzer, a man answered and opened the door, revealing a full-size wire mesh door. Paddy told the man he was there to visit his mother, and the man opened the mesh door and pointed him to a wire mesh window about fifty feet across the room. The scene was surreal for Paddy, and it would be years before he would see the movie *One Flew Over the Cuckoo's Nest* for a reference.

As he approached the window, to his immediate left there was a caged door and to the right a larger area with tables and chairs that appeared to be a community and visiting area. About a dozen people were in the room, some wearing regular clothes and others in white hospital gowns. Paddy told the nurse at the window who he was visiting and was given a few visiting rules and told to find a table or chair to wait at. Paddy nervously made his way to the far side of the room by the windows, found a couple of empty chairs, and waited.

Paddy waited, observing the others in the room while keeping an eye on the wire door by the window. The environment, noise, and an outburst or two from patients helped to increase Paddy's anxiety as he waited for what he felt was a very long time, although in reality, it was probably only ten minutes.

Behind the caged door, a nurse and a patient appeared. A few seconds later, a buzzer sounded, the door swung open, and they entered the room. At first Paddy wasn't sure, but then he recognized the partial growth of his mother's shaved head. Paddy noticed the nurse scanning the room, he stood up and raised his hand, and the nurse approached with his mother. The nurse said something and left. There was no embrace, hugs or kisses, but initially only an awkward silence. They eventually spoke, but Paddy did not remember much about what was said. Eventually the allotted visiting time was up, and the nurse came and walked them across the room. After a brief goodbye hug, his mother and nurse returned through the caged door.

Paddy's visit was depressing. Although his mother's condition seemed better than the last few times he had seen her, what he saw in that room struck him. Paddy found it difficult to describe the scene accurately but experienced a deep sense of empathy for those he had seen. He had seen madness, voidness, sadness, and loneliness in the patients, and hope and loss in visiting family members.

A week later Paddy returned to Bellevue. He made the subway ride, walked the ten blocks, and navigated the maze in Bellevue to the psychiatric ward. He rang the buzzer, entered, and went to the desk and told the nurse who he was visiting.

"Sorry, your mother was discharged a few days ago."

Paddy inquired about where his mother went, and the nurse smiled without any answers for him. Paddy thanked the nurse and left. His initial thought was, *She did it again;*

she left. He wasn't upset or mad, or maybe he was, and repression took over again. He went home and told his dad.

NORMALCY

Normalcy returned for Paddy. School, karate, the subways and buses, and the delivery boy job at D'Agostino's all continued. He was doing well, his repressed memories locked away. His mother's whereabouts unknown for a couple of years until, just like that, she showed up one day. Nothing dramatic, she visited for an hour and later made a few more visits until she moved in. That lasted only a couple of months until one day, when Paddy came home, she was gone, again.

They didn't know where she had moved to. A year or so later, his mother returned again, moved in temporarily, and after a short period, moved out. Paddy suspected those demons probably got ahold of her again.

The Power Memorial Days

After graduating from St. Stephen's, in June of 1972, Paddy went on to attend Power Memorial Academy, a well-known  Catholic high school sports powerhouse in New York City. Power Memorial had a reputation for producing exceptional athletes, many of whom developed into world-class runners, Olympians, professional Hockey, Baseball, and basketball players, as well as a few New York politicians.

Power Memorial was best known for producing several professional NBA players, including one who is famously

known for creating the skyhook shot, Kareem Abdul-Jabbar.

Paddy joined and remained on the track team until January of 1975. The daily after-school track practice in the fall and spring was held at Sheep Meadow in Central Park, just a few blocks from the school.

The path or loop that circled the meadow was about three-quarters of a mile and was the perfect setting for intervals, sprinting, and running laps for distance training. Sheep Meadow was a popular spot for New Yorkers, including celebrities seeking an undisturbed break. On many occasions, the boys would finish a lap sprint and, upon arrival at the end, find a local news anchor or other celebrity sitting on a bench or chatting with the coaches, Brother Bielen, and Brother Smith.

On a few occasions, the runners approached the end of their lap and noticed a gold Rolls Royce parked ahead by the end of the lap. As the boys came to a stop, New York Knicks basketball superstar Walt Frazier was there.

Brother Bielen

Brother Smith

Of course, there was some excitement as Brother Bielen checked his stopwatch and, with a smile, reminded the boys of the two-minute break before the next lap. The two-minute break went by fast with Fraizer complimenting the boys on their performance and briefly conversing with them, which Frazier seemed to enjoy and made future return visits. When the boys completed the next lap, Frazier was still there, and he stayed for the next half hour until practice ended.

The winter indoor track season practice and meets were conducted a subway ride away at an upper Manhattan National Guard Armory, otherwise known as "The Armory." During the summer, there was an opportunity to attend a week long track camp in the Poconos. If you are wondering what you do at a track camp, the answer is you run, run, run. Paddy attended Power for two and a half years through his junior year in January of 1975.

Power Memorial was operated by the Christian Brothers of the Catholic Church. Paddy and other alumni have a strong mutual belief that in addition to education, the Brothers at Power were instrumental in instilling a moral foundation and provided support and guidance. The Brothers lived where they worked, in the upper floors of the Power Memorial building.

The Brothers also maintained what could be considered a safe house in New Jersey, where they helped students in need, experiencing broken homes, and needed a place to stay. Later in this story, at the beginning of January 1975, Paddy consulted Brother Bielen about leaving school to join the Army.

They kept in touch, and after Paddy completed his basic training, he returned to New York on leave in May. A friend from Power offered Paddy a place to stay, and Brother Bielen also made arrangements for Paddy to stay at the safe house, where a few other friends were staying.

Paddy was invited to attend the track team championship meet. The Power track team won the city championship that day and Paddy had the honor to be asked to be part of the team picture.

The friendships, camaraderie, and support, guidance, and moral fortitude that the Christian Brothers provided had an immense positive influence on Paddy and Power alumni.

Power Memorial Academy Track Team - New York — 1975
New York State Catholic Schools Outdoor Team Champions – 1975
New York City CHSAA Outdoor City Champions – 1975

Power Memorial Academy was located at 161 W. 61st Street in Manhattan, a few blocks from Lincoln Center and Fordham University. In 1984, after over 50 years of serving the community, Power Memorial was permanently closed.

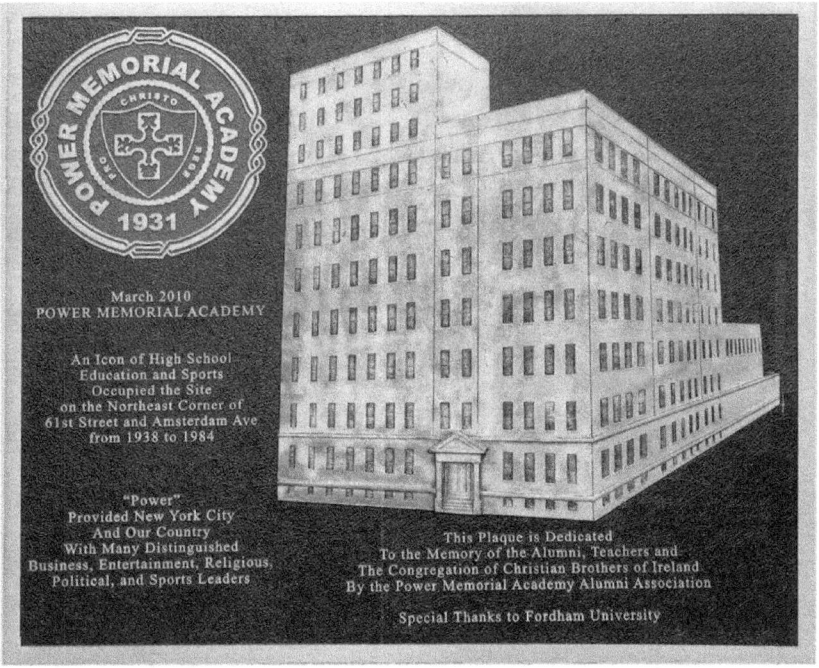

GROWING ACCUSTOMED

Taxi Driver

When Paddy moved in with his dad in 1968, he was working for a shipping company called REA, also known as Railway Express Agency, which ultimately went out of business in 1975. In 1971, Paddy's dad was laid off from REA, and he worked as a taxi driver until the end of 1974. A highlight of the taxi driving period was that his dad was never robbed, which was considered an accomplishment. Another highlight was the celebrities he picked up. There were a lot of celebrities Paddy's dad picked up, and there were several every week. Ed Sullivan stood out due to the popular Ed Sullivan show at the time and he was mentioned most often and was known as a good tipper.

Introvert in Training

Since his arrival in 1967, and more so after moving in with his dad, Paddy had grown accustomed to the streets of New York, traveling the subways and buses, walking to and from school, activities, and events. Activities with friends and school aside, Paddy had an introverted part to his personality, something he would realize later in life and joke about with his writer friends who shared the mystical and often humorous traits of introverts.

Paddy often found himself exploring New York, a habit he developed in Ireland where he randomly walked the roads, farm fields, and countryside for hours—and remember, he even made it to Dublin one time. In Ireland, Paddy had felt there was a limitless world to explore without any apparent restrictions.

After moving in with his dad, Paddy's five block walk to school dramatically changed with a daily Queens to Manhattan commute. Attending school in Manhattan and his delivery boy job expanded Paddy's opportunity to explore. New York City became a limitless world where, between structured activities, he would walk the streets of Manhattan in youthful awe and wonder of the sights and sounds, following his quest for knowledge and zeal for exploration. His ventures took him to the Wall Street area, Times Square, Greenwich Village, Little Italy, every corner of Manhattan, including Harlem, which in hindsight was probably not a good idea for a white kid to explore in the early 1970s.

Museums

Another activity that Paddy had an obsession with was the museums, and New York had two of the best, the Museum of Natural History and the Metropolitan Museum of Art. Paddy lost count of how many times he had visited the museums. One of the wonders that Paddy recalled was that these two museums were enormous, so giant that he could spend half a day or longer exploring them. The opportunity for almost limitless exploration was an attraction for Paddy, and it was an activity he enjoyed doing on his own.

There was one more museum that Paddy found purely

by accident while walking on Fifth Avenue along the edge of Central Park near Eighty-Seven Street. He noticed an oddly shaped white building, and being the curious individual that he was, Paddy crossed the street to the Guggenheim Museum. Upon entering the front door, he was surprised by two things: one, that it was empty, except for a couple of people. The other surprise was what he thought was odd, yet also interesting in appearance, with a large lobby and a spiral ramp that appeared to climb the three-story structure along the walls. Paddy found it fascinating, walked the ramp, and made many return visits.

Combs and Strange Women

During his exploration training in Ireland, Paddy developed a keen skill of observation, which continued to grow in New York, a necessary skill required to survive the city's streets. During the 1960s and 1970s, New York was not known for being a clean city, and trash was abundant on the streets. There was often a variety show of dancing newspaper pages with a supporting cast of varying debris circulating above the sidewalk subway grates.

During the winter and colder months, the subway grates served as a source of warmth for the homeless, who would sit or lie down on them.  These types of observances were common, and depending on the part of the city Paddy was exploring, there were other scenes of both the vibrant and not so vibrant street life composed of an eclectic group of characters, be it peddlers, performers, homeless, drug addicts, prostitutes, and other observations of New York. The Hare Krishnas were a common sight, comprising predominantly young people who dressed in orange robes, had shaved heads, and traveled in groups, handing out pamphlets, and announcing their approach singing "Hare Krishna, Hare Krishna..."

Paddy was always in a state of full observation, aware of his surroundings. He developed a sense, a sense that some might call street smarts. He possessed a radar so to speak, and was able to spot and avoid dangers, potential muggers, and combs. Earlier in Paddy's story, there was mention of combs, and if he saw a comb on the sidewalk or lying on the ground, he would take a deliberate, nervous detour to avoid it and look over his shoulder, just to be sure nothing was there. In hindsight, Paddy found it odd that there were numerous occasions he came across a comb on the sidewalk, even at night. He wondered how a comb would find itself on the sidewalk, and even though it was a question, he did not delay in making his nervous detours.

Prostitutes were a common scene on the streets, and Paddy had mixed memories of his observations. During his explorations, Paddy saw many young and a few older women, who were seemingly alone, standing in doorways or strolling down the sidewalk, none of whom said a word to Paddy, although many of them did cast a smile towards him.

Paddy's first encounter with a prostitute was unexpected and humorous. As he was walking down a street, Paddy was approached by a young woman who said, "Wanna date?" Paddy didn't want to be rude and stopped and smiled. He was polite but found the question odd, especially since he didn't know her. The woman smiled and said, "If you got twenty dollars, we can go on a date." Paddy was unsure what he had said, but he said something that enlightened the woman to his innocence and naivety. The woman smiled and gave Paddy a tap on his shoulder and told him, "Come back and see me when you're a little older, ok." Paddy wasn't rude, smiled, and told the woman, "Ok."

Up until that moment and later reflecting, it had not occurred to Paddy that the women and others he had seen over time were prostitutes. Replays of TV and movie scenes where the "Wanna date" line was used infiltrated his mind.

Paddy was admittedly naive; however, he was learning as he grew older, and certain realities became clear. Repression was still in practice as memories of how his mom's girlfriends dressed and the characteristics they displayed struck him as familiar.

There was another occasion at night after work when Paddy found himself exploring the crowded streets, and as he turned a corner, he observed across the street a young woman standing under a streetlight. At first glance, there was nothing notable, but something about the woman struck Paddy, and he turned his head for a second glance. He was surprised to see the woman crossing the street, walking towards him, and making instant eye contact. A contact that startled Paddy, gave him a chill and caused him to freeze and stop walking. Nervous familiarity overtook Paddy as the redheaded woman approached with a familiar smile that Paddy couldn't quite make out, but yet, familiar. As the woman drew closer, Paddy hesitantly smiled, not sure what he should do as the passersby made comments to Paddy to move out of their way. The woman maintained her smile as she stopped at the curb, kept her smile with what Paddy believed to be green eyes. "You need to turn around...leave and go home."

Paddy was confused and hesitated as he analyzed the woman's comment. Paddy maintained his smile and continued his hesitation, which did not please the woman. The woman stopped smiling and responded sternly, "Go home and stay away from here." Upon hearing the cold stern command from the woman, Paddy made a reluctant turn and began to walk. As he walked, he made a slow, nervous look over his shoulder and was alarmed by the woman standing behind him, "Go home!" she yelled. Paddy sped up his pace and turned the corner.

Paddy never returned to that area of New York and recalled conflicting memories of the incident, wondering if the woman could have been his Guardian Angel. He felt that he might have been too old to believe in Guardian Angels, Banshees, and Reapers, but then again, in hindsight, he knew someone was looking out for him on Forty Second Street in Times Square that night, during a time when the area was crime ridden, filled with X-rated theaters, and prostitution. Yes, surely the Guardian Angel was there that night.

Normalcy and Other Things

Paddy would venture on his own to see movies like *James Bond's Live and Let Die*, *Patton*. and other movies from the late '60s into the early '70s. Upon graduating from St. Stephen's in 1972 and moving on to Power Memorial in the fall, Paddy's social life and most of his school, track, and other activities remained centered in Manhattan.

The daily seventeen-block walk from the apartment on 20th Street in Astoria to the Ditmars subway station was a twenty-minute trek each way. Ditmars was the end of the line for the

RR train that ran through Queens until entering the tunnel under the East River to Manhattan.

Away from Manhattan in Astoria, Paddy attended his karate lessons and was introduced to bowling and coin collection at a coin shop under Ditmars Station. Across the street from the bowling alley and coin shop was the Ditmars movie theater, which by most standards would be considered run down. Ditmars theater was convenient being at the steps of the Ditmars station and cheap to attend a showing. A Google search shows that the theater was converted to a post office in the 1980s.

The Towers

On a Saturday after a track meet in the spring of 1973 or 1974, Paddy talked a couple of his friends into accompanying him on an expedition to the new World Trade Center in lower Manhattan. Upon arrival at the base and looking up at the two towering structures, Paddy was filled with amazement and got the idea of going inside and finding their way to the roof. The first building they tried to enter was locked. They walked to the next building and entered an empty  lobby, a strangely odd sight in itself to find. The emptiness didn't stop them from locating the elevators. They boarded an elevator, which was the biggest elevator any of them had ever seen. They pushed the top floor button, and the elevator took off at a speed with such force that they felt themselves being pushed toward the floor of the elevator.

When the elevator stopped, they got off to find they were only halfway up the tower. They got off to an empty floor, but empty may not be accurate. Although the lobby and offices were devoid of people, various odds and ends of construction tools and buckets were scattered about. One memorable, striking feature was the tall vertical windows that seemed to extend forever. The view was mesmerizing, to say the least for Paddy, and created a lasting memory much like the one he would gain at the next stop on the roof.

After exploring the floor and taking in the view, they found another elevator that went up to the roof with what felt like the speed of a roller coaster. The view of the city from the roof was exhilarating, an unforgettable and fond experience of New York—a memory that would be unexpectedly rekindled on September 11, 2001.

IT'S RAINING MEN

This chapter title may initially jump out as something humorous, and normally it might be, but for Paddy's story, there is a dark side as a sensitive topic is revisited. However, elements of humor might be utilized to aid in deflection and the practice of repression.

This part of Paddy's story was added after the story had been written, edited, and was thought completed. As Paddy has often mentioned, the practice of repression is always in operation, always being refined, revealed, and repressed again. However, recalling his years in New York stirred up many memories for Paddy and won out over repression.

At this point of the story, one might ask what else could there be. The image of raining men may allude to many a thought, and the innocent mind might simply wonder what humorous antidote will be next, while the not-so-innocent, or those experienced in life and its unfairness and cruelties, might have already predicted where this part of the story is going.

Paddy's story for the most part has been in chronological sequence except for when covering overlapping experiences. This part of Paddy's story also overlaps some previous parts and covers the period of 1970 through of fall of 1974.

Midnight Cowboy

Movie theaters in New York in the 1970s did not appear  to enforce age restrictions for rated R movies, or movies that had an X rating and were changed to an R rating, like the 1969 X-rated Oscar winner *Midnight Cowboy* that had a rating change to R in 1971.

Paddy fell victim to the hype and allure of an Oscar-winning, once X- turned R-rated movie. He nervously approached the ticket window at Ditmars theater and was surprised that he was not asked for ID, and barely even noticed by the attendant. There were about a dozen others in the theater, and as the movie played, the fourteen-year-old Paddy failed to understand what all the fuss was about concerning the movie.

Up to this point in Paddy's life, Paddy was extremely shy, his experience with girls was limited—a couple of innocently shy girlfriend encounters, a few almost dates—and not at all sexually experienced. Sex was, like for most young teenagers, forbidden, strange, confusing, frustrating, and any other descriptions that tend to belong to teenage pubescence in addition to the well-known Catholic guilt associated with sex.

The following part of Paddy's story is similar to other young teenagers' stories whose innocence is stolen, yet uniquely different for each individual victim. Graphic details are not necessary to illustrate what happened to Paddy when a man sat down in the seat next to him, placed his hand on Paddy's lap, and moments later lowered his head. Paddy's attempt to leave and resist was physically and verbally stopped.

There is a common response about certain situations people find themselves in when they say they didn't know what to do. That was Paddy's reaction to this situation. Undefined emotions, confusion, naivety, lack of understanding, frustration, and a conglomerate of other feelings overwhelmed Paddy after the man left, and the first seed of hate was planted.

Paddy stayed for the rest of the movie and pretended nothing had happened as his mind raced with the unifying emotional roller coaster that victims share as he reengaged the art of repression and forgetting. The process of repression was helped in large part near the end of the movie with the appearance of what Paddy saw as a cute and beautiful actress Brenda Vaccaro. He developed an instant infatuation for the actress; there was something about her face and smile he found unforgettable.

After the movie on his way home, Paddy had an afterthought: *My Guardian Angel didn't save me today.* Paddy never returned to the Ditmars theater, and being an experienced practitioner of repression, he never told anyone and forgot about the Ditmars incident for over fifty years until he wrote down his story.

The Uniquely Gay 1970s

The 1970s was a unique time in New York and the rest of the country for men in the gay community, a community that fell victim to being classified into several negative stereotypes, some unfair and untruthful, and others brought about by a segment of the gay community that could be defined by bad or criminal behavior.

During the later 1960s into the 1970s, the brashness of some gay men seemed to have no boundaries. It was a common scene in New York, which Paddy witnessed, to see gay men performing oral sex on each other in the corners of subway stations, on the subways, back of buses, or in alleys, stairwells, and entrances to buildings. There was no limit or restraint to their public exhibitionism.

The Gallery Gay Man

One Saturday afternoon in 1972, or maybe a year earlier or later, Paddy was working his delivery job at D'Agostino's and made a grocery delivery to an art gallery. The gallery was between Lexington and Park Avenues on 70 Something Street. Paddy was greeted by a man at the gallery, and as customary for deliveries, Paddy made multiple trips inside, carrying bags of groceries to a second-floor kitchenette. Upon bringing the last few bags inside, the customary tip was presented, and Paddy said thank you and started to leave.

Just as in the movie theater incident, graphic details are not needed to detail how as Paddy walked across the dimly lit gallery area, he found himself forcibly overpowered, face down on the floor and pinned. The forceful assault lasted five minutes. Upon completion, Paddy found the man to suddenly be pleasant, apologizing if he hurt Paddy, and politely shown to the bathroom. As Paddy left the gallery, the man acted like they were friends and gave Paddy another tip. There was a lot of psychology in play on the part of the man, and probably on Paddy too, which Paddy learned years later about how predators act. The second seed of hate was planted, and again an afterthought occurred to Paddy: *My Guardian Angel didn't save me again.*

Southern Exposure

Earlier in Paddy's story, he mentioned his participation on his high school track team and their daily practice sessions in Central Park in the fall and spring. The practice schedule alternated between sessions at Sheep Meadow and days when the distance runners ran for about an hour through the park, taking them through trails heading north around the Central Park Reservoir and up to the northern edge of the park at 110th Street.

As the boys made their way through varying paths, many were secluded by trees, brushes, and boulders. On one occasion, two of the boys were ahead of the group when a man literally jumped out from behind a tree, exposing himself to them. They presumed he was a gay man based on known stereotypes and the man's actions, dress, body language, and comments he made.

As soon as the rest of the group of runners approached, the man executed a panicked escape. This was one of the numerous times this type of situation occurred. On another occasion, a similar occurrence happened where two of the runners were ahead of the group and a different man jumped out from behind a large boulder.

Men jumping out from behind trees and rocks sounds like it could be a scene in a movie musical instead of actually happening. The same exposure repeated itself, and the boys joked about these incidents and how it seemed that all the gay men around the city had shared the same script directing them on the who, what, when, where, and what to say when performing their lurid actions. Paddy had a distinct memory of one incident when, as in other episodes, a man jumped from behind a boulder, wearing tight white pants, and exposed himself. As scripted, the man remained exposed for a few seconds until the trailing group of runners approached, at which time he zipped up and started his escape.

However, on that day, the script writer had not prepared the actor for the highly skilled verbalizations that a few Catholic high school boys could unleash. Paddy and the others watched two of the runners begin their verbal orchestration of derogatory, bigoted slurs and threats bombarded at the escaping man, who at first began a quick walk. However, looking over his shoulder at the two connoisseurs of the English language propelling their expletives as they sprinted in his direction, the man executed what must have been an instinctive plan B, which began as a slow run, followed seconds later—upon seeing the runners' distance close—by an accelerated run.

In that moment, the man in his tight white pants instinctively felt the immediate necessity for self-preservation. This entire moment covered only a few seconds, but Paddy could see the fear in the man's face as he darted by and ran down the hill with the two boys angrily in pursuit. The incident occurred near a part of the path that crested the top of a hill with an overview of a large field that stretched about half a mile to the west edge of the park.

The chase continued then disappeared out of sight as the rest of the runners made an impromptu stop, joking and wondering where their two friends were. After a minute or two passed, one of the boys yelled out, "Look!" He pointed down to the field where the distinctive pair of white pants and its occupant were racing across the field toward the edge of the park, pursued by two high school boys, who were allowing the man to escape the park. Surely it was on purpose because how could two high school track stars not catch a man running for his life. While chasing a gay man out of the park may have seemed like a joking matter to the boys, Paddy's hindsight would realize it was wrong...although not as wrong as what the man had done.

Years later, as Paddy grew older, and experienced life, to include having gay friends and coworkers, even in the Army, his negative view of gay men would change. Paddy included the park incidents in his story not for pity or forgiveness, or to justify his youthful learned hatred and bigotry toward gay men, but more so to demonstrate how young impressionable minds can be influenced by what they witness and experience—especially in his case, being molested and assaulted by gay men. His initial view was reinforced by the exhibitionist displays of a select group of gay men in the parks and other places throughout the city.

Paddy's personal experiences taught him to believe the stereotype that all gay men were child-molesting pedophiles, a false stereotype that sadly was widely believed in society. Paddy later learned that perceptions can be wrong, and the same application of witnessing and having positive experiences can also change perceptions and beliefs. Since the 1970s, it became well-known and documented time and again that perversion and pedophilia does not infect a specific group or segment within a society, and the statistics have shown that the majority of pedophiles are straight men. Unfortunately, just like liars believe their own lies, the bigoted often continue to believe their own bigotry and hate.

CONSEQUENCE AND DESTINY

Near the end of 1974, Paddy's mother showed up for another temporary stay. Those demons were at work again, and after a short stay, she moved out again. His dad's repeated attempts to help Paddy's mother caused emotional torment that took a toll on Paddy's dad, including a bout of depression, which led to unemployment and other circumstances that created a situation where they were no longer able to remain in the apartment.

Options were discussed. Paddy asked advice from Brother Bielen, who offered an opportunity for Paddy to reside in a home for boys that the Christian Brothers operated. Paddy appreciated Brother Bielen's offer but ultimately decided that joining the Army was the best option, which, in hindsight, was influenced in part by his dad and by an Army and Marine Corps recruiter.

The Recruiters

Paddy visited a Marine recruiter, a decision inspired by a "We Don't Promise You a Rose Garden" Marine Corps

television commercial featuring a popular song titled "Rose Garden." His interview may not have been the best and resulted in what Paddy believed to be the biggest mistake in the Marine Corps' history. The Marine recruiter escorted Paddy across the hall to the Army recruiter. Nonverbal communication and whispers were exchanged between the recruiters. The Marine turned and left the room, leaving Paddy with the Army recruiter, who studied the self-assured non–high school grad. The Army recruiter must have seen something, maybe a shortcoming of some kind or perhaps he recognized something else, a hidden quality in Paddy, the future Green Beret.

The next step a few days later was taking the entrance test. The recruiter drove Paddy and several others to a testing center where over a hundred young volunteers were assembled to take the written aptitude test that would take up to three hours to complete. After the testing was over, the waiting game began. The volunteers waited for over half an hour until several Army sergeants entered the room.

"When we call out your name, stand up and go out to the hallway and see the sergeants out there."

The long process of calling out names proceeded for half an hour as one by one, names were called, volunteers stood up, smiling with pride at their accomplishment of passing the test, and walked out of the room. Time dragged on as the names were called, and Paddy grew anxious hoping his name would be called next. Paddy exchanged concerned glances with a few others as the numbers in the room dwindled until there were only a few remaining, around eight or ten, including Paddy.

The sergeant stopped calling out names, looked around, and left the room, which generated a wave of disappointment within Paddy and the others. Paddy had a distinct memory of one of the young men starting to cry. A few minutes later, the sergeant came back into the room and the conversations ceased. The sergeant looked around the room and smiled.

"Congratulations...you passed. All those guys out there in the hallway failed the test... The National Guard and Reserve recruiters are talking to them."

Paddy joined the Army in January of 1975, left New York, and was on his way to Fort Polk, Louisiana, where he began his twenty-one-year career in the Army.

Any other story like this one might normally end here with a young man joining the Army, having a career in the Army, getting married, having children and grandchildren, transitioning to business, earning an MBA and Ph.D., teaching college, becoming an Author, and living happily ever after. A regular story might end that way, but not this one. Paddy's story does not end here because of a lingering question you may have asked yourself or wondered about. What happened with Paddy's sister back in Ireland in 1967?

MOTHER'S CHOICE

The circumstances on how Paddy returned to the United States with his mother and how that transpired is a story in itself. The visit to Bellevue, subsequent temporary stays by his mother, and his dad's depression were difficult for Paddy; however, this part of Paddy's story—Banshees and repressions aside—was the most difficult for Paddy to reflect on.

Before his return to the United States, back in Ireland in 1967, Paddy's mother arrived a few weeks after his escape attempt to Dublin. Whether that visit had been scheduled or was prompted by the escape attempt, Paddy did not know, but he was overjoyed to see his mother, and there was no mention of the runaway episode to Dublin. The visit lasted about two weeks, during which Paddy spent time with his mother and sister, returned to his daily adventures, and spent a few nights at Butler's Pub watching his mother sing and play the accordion. Life was idyllic for Paddy at this time, and repressed memories were locked away, locked away forever, until...

Early on an overcast, dreary morning, a car pulled up outside the house, just as it had frequently done since his mother's return. His mother usually drove the car, but on that morning, a man drove. Paddy did not take much notice and went about his morning with his sister.

As the minutes passed, Paddy observed quiet conversations between Aunt Joe and his mother, more so than usual. A familiar sense returned to Paddy as his mother, who appeared anxious, checked and double-checked her handbag. Paddy recognized the pattern, as he had previously seen it on several occasions just before his mother walked out of the house and got into a car.

It was happening again—his mother nervously preparing to leave without him. Paddy observed her closely to make sure he was right about the pattern. He wanted to be sure while wishing it was not, but it was. The final clue was the last step in the pattern when his mother opened her wallet, took money out, and handed it to Aunt Joe.

Paddy walked outside to the black four-door car, opened the back door, got in, and left the door open, providing a full view of the front door of the house. He was overwhelmed by emotions, enraged with the thought of his mother leaving. He positioned himself against the opposite-side back door to watch the open door of the house and waited. Aunt Joe briefly entered the doorway, saw Paddy in the car, and went back inside.

A few minutes later, Paddy's mother and Aunt Joe walked out the front door and hugged, and then his mother picked up his sister and give her a kiss and set her back down on the ground. With tears in her eyes, his mother walked to the car, leaned in, and asked Paddy to come out to give her a hug and kiss. Paddy stubbornly refused. He sat in the corner with his arms folded.

"Take me with you, take me with you! I'm not staying here. Take me with you!"

A heartbreaking session of pleading and begging ensued. Paddy had learned from the previous departures of his mother and Uncle Jimmy, and this time, he was determined to not be left behind. Attempts by his mother to grab and pull Paddy from the car were no match for the begging, kicking, and screaming Paddy. Determined, his mind was set; nothing was stopping him from going with his mother. The crying and begging continued, and to Paddy, it felt like a timeless moment, one that would be etched in his mind forever—not because he was left behind but because of what happened next.

His mother made another attempt to remove Paddy from the car without success. She was frustrated and crying and stepped back. She turned and walked back to the house and talked with Aunt Joe. She went inside for a minute and came back to the doorway, giving Aunt Joe a hug and Paddy's sister another hug and kiss goodbye. Paddy was still crying and watched his mother approach the car when she unexpectedly closed the back door and got in the front seat next to the driver. Paddy's mother sternly told the driver, "Let's go."

Paddy worked on controlling his tantrum, taking in what was happening and unsure what it meant. He felt a slight shift of the car as the driver put it in gear. Paddy looked out the window at his sister standing next to Aunt Joe holding her hand. Aunt Joe was clutching her apron with her other hand, tears in her eyes. Paddy realized what was happening, and he began begging and pleading with his mother to wait and get his sister. Paddy's mother issued another command to the driver: "Keep going." The car kept moving, and Paddy slid over to the other window, screaming, "Don't leave her, don't leave her! Please, Mommy, don't leave her!"

That surreal moment felt like it was happening in slow motion. His sister was expressionless as she watched the car drive away, too young to understand, but Aunt Joe cried as she watched them pull away. When the house was out of sight, Paddy sat back, sulked, and continued his pleas to go back and get his sister. His sulking and crying eventually stopped, and the only words spoken that Paddy remembered were between his mother and the driver. Paddy's thoughts traveled aimlessly; he was emotionally drained. He thought about his sister but gave not a thought about leaving without anything, not a suitcase or anything—literally leaving with only the clothes on his back in an apparent last-minute decision by his mother, brought on by the emotional tirade of her son to make a choice, a mother's choice, a heart-wrenching choice to leave one child behind and take the other one.

No words were spoken between Paddy and his mother during the drive to Shannon Airport. As they were nearing the airport, Paddy watched his mother do something that to this day he did not understand, although one could speculate why she tore part of a page out of a passport.

That morning, a glance through the car window was the last time his mother and sister ever saw each other and the last time his mother ever saw her mother, Aunt Joe. It would be decades before Paddy and his sister would see each other again; however, when his sister grew older, they began to write letters to each other.

EPILOGUE

Their mother made a choice. The rationale, aside from an emotional heat-of-the-moment decision prompted by Paddy's outburst, was likely to do with Paddy had a passport while his sister did not, and their mother believed that she would be able to arrange to bring his sister to the States later. Paddy remembered conversations with his mother about bringing his sister to the States, which didn't happen— not from lack of effort, love, or best intentions, but from unfortunate circumstances and demons that invaded their mother's life.

Years later after successful repression on Paddy's part, he grasped the gravity of the love and guilt-driven decision his mother made, and he experienced overwhelming guilt about leaving his sister behind. Paddy realized that the only reason he was able to leave Ireland was due to his emotionally charged outburst that guilted his mother into taking him. Despite the guilt, Paddy knew if he had remained in Ireland, both he and his sister would have different lives and would not have ended up with the families, children, and grandchildren they have—all blessings despite life's hardships, heartache, and Paddy's guilt.

Paddy and his sister knew their mother loved them and had the best intentions. They understood that it was no fault of their mother that demons in New York City had latched their clutches onto her.

If Paddy were asked the question if he would change anything, even the incidents that occurred in New York, he would answer, "No." His reason would be because to change one thing would result in absolutely voiding the blessings of his and his sister's children and grandchildren. Although Paddy was disappointed with his Guardian Angel for not saving him from the assaults in New York, he still believes he has a Guardian Angel watching over him and his family, just like he has the Banshee, always nearby, lingering and waiting with its companion, the Grim Reaper.

The Metaphorical Banshee

Sigmund Freud has been quoted as saying that the Irish are impervious to psychoanalysis. Given that Paddy is Irish, he may fit the characterization, however, imperviousness aside, a psychological evaluation of Paddy might conclude that a metaphor was in play with Paddy's imagination and his encounters with the Banshee and Reaper. The use of a metaphorical Banshee and Grim Reaper could be representative of the guilt experienced for leaving his sister. Aside from that, the Banshee part of Paddy's story is a good and entertaining Banshee story to add to the myths.

Paddy decided to share his story and experiences as an example for those who experienced a broken home or some form of abuse or hardship during their childhoods. Paddy's example shows that stereotypes and cycles that so many find themselves falling into can be broken and overcome.

Emotions and feelings inevitably cannot be avoided; however, the seeds of hate, bigotry, and guilt can be changed, and victims can overcome the challenges they have endured. They can live happy and repression-free lives, if they choose to do so. The victims of childhood heartaches can be absolved of the sentence of the undeserving, faultless guilt they have endured.

When we began Paddy's story, it was mentioned that Paddy was born in 1956 to be a fearless, mischievous, curious, and easily influenced young boy. Despite his tendency to be attracted to what others may find harmful, or even outright dangerous, in addition to the known precarious circumstances of his life, he experienced a lifetime of what some might consider angelic protection, even into adulthood.

Paddy believes that everyone has a Guardian Angel, a Banshee, and a Reaper in their lives waiting for their respective opportunities to do their jobs, and despite the unfortunate events in Paddy's life, he believes the Guardian Angel has done a far better job than the competition. After reading Paddy's story, you may not believe in Banshees and Grim Reapers, or maybe you do, but at the very least, you've got to believe in Guardian Angels.

"Don't let the bad days win"

"Be yourself; everyone else is already taken." — Oscar Wilde

ABOUT THE AUTHOR

The use of the classic Irish name Paddy in this story is a pseudonym for Marty Martin (Warren, Pop Pop, Dr. Martin). He has many names, and after his return from Ireland, he was given the nickname "Irish" due to his accent at the time. He grew up in New York City, where he attended St. Stephen's of Hungary Elementary School and Power Memorial Academy High School. Marty joined the Army in 1975 where he served twenty-one years. He met his wife Debbie and they had three wonderful children and were a globetrotting military family. During his career in the Army, Marty served in the Infantry, Military Police and caught the bug to jump out of perfectly good airplanes and volunteered for Special Forces (*Green Berets*).

After retiring from the Army in 1996, Marty transitioned to business, working for Domino's Pizza Corporation and later a Domino's franchise business owner. Marty earned his Ph.D. in Business Administration and Organizational Leadership from North Central

University and an MBA from the University of Michigan (*Go Blue*). He transitioned to teaching at Bryan University, Norwich University, and Southern New Hampshire University.

Marty is an award-winning writer of fiction, non-fiction, and Children's books. As a Grandparent he has a Children's book series based on his experiences with his grandchildren "Adventures with Pop Pop".

He is a member of numerous writing organizations including the St. Louis Writers' Guild, Sisters in Crime, the Military Writers Society of America, and has served as President of the Missouri Writers' Guild and the St. Louis Publishers Association.

In 2022, Marty suffered a stroke and wrote a book about the recovery and rehabilitation process and provides guidance and support to Stroke victims and their families.

Marty lives with his wife Debbie Kay in St. Louis, Missouri.

You can learn more about Marty and all his books and audiobooks at his website Martymartin.net

Marty Martin Website